W9-BEY-166

Awaken Your Body, Balance Your Mind

Awaken Your Body, Balance Your Mind

Perfect Health
Using the Chi
Ball Method

Thorsons

Monica Linford

with Jennai Cox

Thorsons
An Imprint of HarperCollins*Publishers*
77–85 Fulham Palace Road
Hammersmith, London W6 8JB

The Thorsons website address is: www.thorsons.com

Published by Thorsons 2000

10 9 8 7 6 5 4 3 2 1

© Monica Linford 2000

Monica Linford asserts the moral right to be
identified as the author of this work

A catalogue record for this book
is available from the British Library

ISBN 0 7225 3993 2

Printed in Great Britain by
The Bath Press, Bath

Pilates® is a registered trademark of Sean Gallagher in the USA.
Many of the designations used by manufacturers and sellers to distinguish
their products are claimed as trademarks. Where those designations appear
in this book and Thorsons was aware of a trademark claim, the designations
have been printed in initial capital letters.

contents

In 1993 I decided to commit myself fully to a lifetime of personal study and practice of the most profound philosophies and exercise disciplines of both the East and West. An entire book could be dedicated to the countless people who have offered their professional advice, personal support, unconditional love and friendship during these early years of learning. In particular I would like to extend my utmost gratitude and thanks to:

Julie Toyama – a dear and valuable friend, for your example, all those years ago, of teaching from the heart with humility and passion.

Nicole Brammy at Precinct Physiotherapy in Adelaide, for bringing to my attention the latest research in back care and impressing upon me that simplicity in exercise is always the best option.

My dear friend Alex Rees, for your example of perseverance, courage, inner strength and determination. Your consistent friendship and professional support for more than 10 years will always be appreciated.

Diana and Phil Jaquillard, for your professional services and friendship.

Steve Hardacre, for your wonderful sense of humour and kind support as photographer and friend when budgets were tight.

Brent and Jane Hallo at Fitness Professionals Education, for your recognition, endorsements and encouragement for nearly 10 years in the fitness industry.

Dean Taylor, for your invaluable role as friend and companion during five particularly challenging years of study. Much of my recovery from Chronic Fatigue Syndrome I attribute to your kindness, immense patience and understanding, which will always be appreciated.

Michael Porter and John Wigg for awakening my body, and Surya Silva and Michael Domeyko-Rowland, whose work awakened and balanced my mind.

Jennai Cox, for your friendship and outstanding talent as a journalist, writer and editor and for recognizing the value of Chi Ball Method as a unique exercise system when it was still in its infancy. I am indebted to you as my ghost editor and writer, for keeping me on track during those very challenging days of writing this manuscript.

Jennifer Harper for being a key catalyst in making this book possible and for leading me to such a wonderfully supportive team at Thorsons.

acknowledgements

Wanda Whiteley at Thorsons for gently nudging me in the right direction as I wrote my first manuscript, and Barbara Vesey for her sympathetic and professional eye in the final editing process.

All the people who have become enthusiastic practitioners and teachers of the Chi Ball Method, especially my original students and participants in Adelaide, Australia – I thank you for your endorsements, feedback and testimonials. These invaluable comments have helped promote further research and development for an exercise system which endeavours to suit and benefit all.

To darling Nigel for sustaining me with so much love, emotional support and countless inspirational conversations. Thank you for reminding me to be all-embracing and fully awake to life and its many choices.

Finally, my dear parents, Tony and Elaine Linford. Much of what I have achieved to this point in my life would not have been possible without your love and invaluable support. Thank you from the bottom of my heart.

Publishers' Note

Monica Linford's Chi Balls are available via mail order (see details on page **209**).

If you do not wish to use a Chi Ball, it is still beneficial to do the exercises – and in most cases a small towel can be substituted for the Chi Ball.

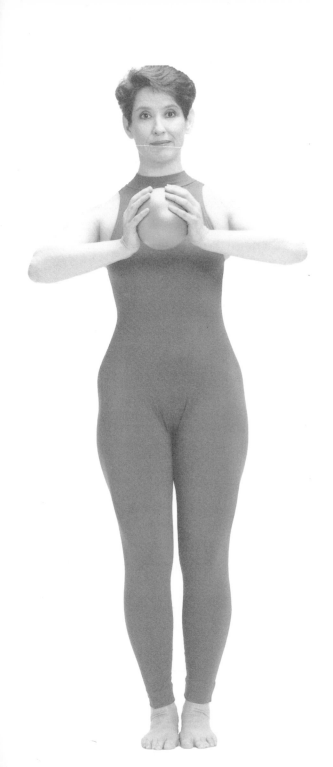

introduction

true fitness, inside and out

When you are filled with stress and fear, then the cells of your body don't respond the way they are supposed to. Sometimes they become stagnant and don't respond at all. When that happens, you have real problems.

Mastering Miracles, Dr Hong Liu

Through often bitter experience many of us come to realize that achieving good health and fitness goes beyond food and exercise. Having adopted as our own society's expectations of how we should look, increasing numbers of us follow punishing fitness programmes and rigid diets, having 'fat days' and 'thin days' while worrying constantly about the amounts we eat and exercise. When we fail to eat less or exercise more, as often we do, depression sets in, so a routine intended to rid us of dissatisfaction with ourselves only leaves us feeling worse.

Fear, therefore, is the emotion that motivates many to exercise. Fear of never having the ideal body shape, fear of having a high cholesterol count, or fear of dying from a heart attack. Too few people today exercise because it feels good or is fun, and any activity motivated by the feelings of low self-worth – which drive so many into the gym or to run round the block – actually does our overall health far more harm than good.

So, as difficult for some as it might be, the first step to successfully achieving true good health is to make our priority the way we *feel* and not how we look. An obsession with physical appearance and a disregard for the internal functioning of the body simply degenerates into bad health, both inside and out.

Because we are rarely ever really satisfied with our body, we can feel hostile and resentful towards it and this, along with other negative emotions, also adversely affects our organs. If these cannot work properly we will never look, let alone feel, truly well.

Anger and frustration at being unable to lose weight damages the liver, yo-yo dieting (eating nothing for one week, than overeating the next) puts great strain on the stomach, spleen and intestines, and excessive exercising drains energy required for the kidneys to work. As the body is pushed further and further off balance, it will, in desperation, store fat for survival. The feelings of depression that result because of our preoccupation with our shape put further strain on our metabolism, making the problem even worse.

Staying Well

Exercise can and should be a means by which to stay well. It is a form of treatment completely in our control that can be used to stay well or heal the body when we are sick. With the right exercises, and taking into consideration other factors affecting our lives such as stress, diet and environment, we can rejuvenate and bring balance back into the body by improving the function of our central nervous system, inner organs, muscles, tissues, ligaments and tendons. We give it an inner as well as outer workout.

If we can exercise from this perspective, with our physical health foremost in our minds, our physical appearance tends naturally to readjust itself. As our metabolism settles the body finds a weight at which it can function properly, and as exercise helps calm our minds, this is usually a weight we find ourselves content with.

This is, of course, a long way from the attitude taken by the majority in the West. Statistics indicate that only between 10 and 20 per cent of the population exercise on a regular basis. Many are put off by early experiences of sport at school, and in later life associate any sort of physical exertion with whatever was felt at that time.

In the introduction to his book *Body, Mind and Sport*, John Douillard, a former professional athlete who, in order to find a way of matching people with the right physical activity, studied India's Ayurvedic medicine, points out that the first experience of failure for 50 per cent of American children is on a sports field.

The root of the problem, I believe, is that exercise is not fun. It is a WORKout, based on the theory that in order to build up the body, you must first break it down ... The key lies in the opposite approach. Increased mind–body integration is the secret ingredient for an enjoyable, safe fitness programme that can last for the rest of your life.

John Douillard, *Body, Mind and Sport*

According to Ayurveda – which means 'Science of Life' – there are three distinct body types: Vata are the speedy, highly strung, very thin racehorse types (such as sprinters, gymnasts and ballet dancers); Pitta are the high achievers of medium build, the competitive team captains (such as tennis players, rock climbers, contemporary/modern dancers, martial artists, basketball players and runners); Kapha are the more stocky, slow types (such as bodybuilders, shot-putters, javelin- and discus-throwers). Most of us are a mixture of two or even all three types, but will be predominantly either Vata, Pitta or Kapha.

The Chi Ball Method

Exercise should be more like a game. If we are going to want to play more often, we should leave feeling not exhausted and drained, but uplifted both physically and emotionally.

What makes the Chi Ball Method truly unique is its alignment with Traditional Chinese Medicine (TCM), which has within its philosophy for health two concepts of balance – yin and yang – and the Five Elements theory. Through these concepts we can learn a simple but profound way in which we can begin to balance our health.

Integrating the Chi Ball Method exercises with TCM follows the higher purpose of Tai Chi, Chi Kung and Yoga, which aim to cleanse, rejuvenate and refresh the inner body so that the outer body can reflect radiant and harmonious health.

The Chi Ball Method concentrates on feeling good.

It appeals to and is designed for all ages and physical abilities. It is fun, playful and concentrates the mind without us even having to try.

Fast-track, high-powered fitness regimes, undertaken by so many of us, are often a reflection of the pace of our lives. If our lives are punishingly stressful, we will often, perhaps subconsciously, choose a fitness regime to match.

Because our minds are already overburdened with information and worry, many of us have great difficulty concentrating on one thing for any significant length of time. We find slow exercise regimes abhorrent, and are daunted by the concentration and commitment required to do the more purist forms of Tai Chi, Chi Kung, Yoga, Body Conditioning, Feldenkrais and Deep Relaxation.

Overcoming these apparent difficulties holds the key to reversing or bringing balance to a stressful existence. Many of the forms of exercise named above are now recommended to those who suffer stress-related illnesses. Here, again, is the concept of balance. With the Chi Ball

Method I have tried to create a simple, gentle and varied exercise programme mixing ancient and more recently developed mind/body exercises. The moves are not unfamiliar, but the results in your breathing, energy levels and ability to relax certainly will be.

My Own Path to Chi Ball

Superior treatment consists of dealing with an illness before it appears; mediocre treatment consists of curing an illness on the point of revealing itself; inferior treatment consists of curing the illness once it has manifested itself.

5th-century Chinese physician Sun Simiao

In 1991, while on holiday in Australia, I was diagnosed with Chronic Fatigue Syndrome (or ME). At the time I was a 'fit and healthy' exercise instructor and presenter working predominantly in the UK. My life was fast-paced and highly stressful, with little or no time for relaxation. I declared to friends and colleagues who suggested I needed some rest that I was far too busy and could not possibly afford the time.

From the latter part of the late 1980s I had been plagued with frequent colds and flu and was constantly injuring myself and, in spite of the highly energetic classes I taught, often lacked energy to do anything else. I put the fluctuations in my energy levels and my growing vulnerability to colds, sprains or other pains down to the weather or hard work.

I did nothing about the frequent bouts of ill-health, and in the three years preceding my ME diagnosis the symptoms progressively worsened. Despite being an expert in all the latest health- and fitness-related research and techniques, I lived from day to day in complete ignorance of my own physical limitations, unaware of the true state of my own health and well-being.

Then, in June 1990, halfway through taking a highly energetic aerobics masterclass, I felt an alarming pain. It shot through the right side of my neck and head, leaving me without feeling and completely paralysed down that side of my body. I carried on teaching, giving hand signals with my left side, never for a moment even considering that I should stop the class.

Once the class had left and some feeling had returned to my right side, I decided to go home, but was so drained I could barely walk down the stairs. It was as though someone had turned off my life switch and pulled out the plug. I was admitted by a doctor to hospital the following day, where an MRI scan and ECG test ruled out a suspected stroke.

Despite never having experienced even the slightest headache, during my collapse I was diagnosed with migraine and sent home with betablockers for the pain. Determined not to allow this 'glitch' in my health to spoil my chances of success I carried on working harder than ever, in preparation for a huge convention for which I had received considerably high-profile sponsorship. Huge abscesses that began to appear under my arm and in my groin could not even derail me from my gruelling work schedule.

Having ignored all the warning signs that my entire body was in crisis, I was finally brought to a complete standstill in September 1992 by an enormous abscess behind my left knee. Within 48 hours my leg had swelled to double its normal size and I found myself in hospital undergoing emergency surgery to have the abscess drained.

While lying in the recovery room a doctor appeared. 'You have a hole in your leg 1½ inches deep and 2 inches wide. It has taken us two hours to drain it. Whatever you are angry about, go and sort it out.' His words helped change my life. It was the first time it had occurred to me that my health was in crisis and that I had contributed to being in this state. Chinese medicine says that we often receive warning of disharmony six to nine months prior to an illness revealing itself. How often do we ignore our body's irritating 'niggles'?

To recover from the operation and get back some of my strength, I folded my business and returned to live full-time in Australia. Once back home in Adelaide, I was by fortune introduced to a practitioner of Chinese medicine, Michael Porter, who diagnosed what is known in the West as Chronic Fatigue Syndrome, or ME. Michael explained that in his stream of medical practice ME is referred to as a depletion of our living energy (the Chinese call it *chi*). In order to treat me he would have to try to find out what had caused the gradual erosion of my chi.

The part played by our emotions in health, only now (slowly) being acknowledged by Western medicine, was one of the significant contributing factors in my deterioration. Much can be achieved by correcting the physical symptoms of an illness, but if we fail to address the effect of excessive emotional states we continue to sabotage our health.

Michael went on to explain the connection between the health of the mind and that of the body. Just as recovering from an illness makes us feel better emotionally, learning how to heal the emotions can have a dramatic effect on our bodies. Because the mind is usually overactive, one of the many symptoms of CFS is an inability to get a good night's sleep, in spite of being completely exhausted during the day. Most nights for me passed in restless tossing and turning, and when I did wake up it was with a headache and without the will or energy to get out of bed.

Michael suggested that I take gentle, non-strenuous Yoga classes and learn to sit still with my eyes closed for 10 to 20 minutes twice a day (to meditate, in other words), which would make me aware of just how overburdened my mind really was. It was torture. All the emotions I had denied feeling or expressing came bubbling up. Guilt, frustration, anger, fear, disappointment, shame and anxiety were among the first to surface. Their suppression, I know now, had been a powerful drain on my energy and contributed to the ME.

After six months of acupuncture, Chinese herbal medicine and Michael's recommended routine of Yoga and meditation, my energy levels began to return. The Yoga and meditation required enormous discipline and determination, and seemed in some ways more like punishment than recovery. But gradually I was able simply to sit in silence for longer and longer, eventually managing half an hour without effort.

The change in my personality, levels of energy and overall state of health over the next three years was profound. I learned how to be aware of my emotions and that I could control them instead of allowing them to control me. More often than not I was able to face challenges or personal crises in a calm and detached manner, and not become stressed, worried or filled with foreboding.

I also became highly sensitive to my energy levels. Symptoms of overdoing any physical activity were (and still, albeit very rarely, are) feverishness, sore and tender muscles, aching joints, headaches, the inability to concentrate and a severe drop in my energy levels. Instead of ignoring or dismissing these signs, I immediately sit still for 20 minutes and do some gentle breathing exercises, soon after which I can feel my energy levels begin to lift.

After a year of pretty rigid adherence to this routine I went from being able to do virtually nothing to working four to six hours a day before lethargy or fatigue set in.

I have come to believe that CFS sufferers feel immense guilt and frustration, and as this takes hold of their health depression sets in, sitting above them like a big black cloud. In the resulting state of hopelessness and helplessness recovery seems impossible, and so the vicious circle continues.

The key to my recovery was to allow these feelings space for expression. Trying to avoid the illness or pretend it was not there and looking in desperation for some kind of 'quick fix' only made it stronger. Accepting the condition brought a huge sense of relief and marked the beginning of my recovery. I was no longer wasting energy on fighting with myself, but regaining it to fight the illness.

Developing the Chi Ball Method

While treating and advising me, Michael made it clear that in Traditional Chinese Medicine it is vital that the patient play a part in his or her own healing. In addition to taking plenty of rest, meditating and going to two Yoga classes a week, I ate only healthy and nutritious home-cooked food. Before meditating I also walked for up to 15 minutes to stimulate the circulation of both my blood and chi.

It seemed an almost natural transition, when I returned six months later to teaching twice a week, to integrate the Eastern philosophy of how to balance energy in the body into my classes. I was struck almost immediately with the way the principles of health as laid out in Traditional Chinese Medicine could be imported perfectly into exercise classes.

Balance is achieved when we follow vigorous exercising with Deep Relaxation. Moving and stretching the body for a while, which stimulates circulation and encourages energy to flow to all our inner organs, is followed by Deep Relaxation or Meditation, which calms and consolidates the energy in the body and the mind.

Fuelled by enthusiasm I began incorporating Deep Relaxation techniques into my classes. Many voted with their feet and left, but this only made me realize they were a reflection of myself a few years previously – unable just to be still and relax.

Similarly, when I tried to integrate the slow and subtle moves from the Feldenkrais Method, an exercise I had come across during my recovery that helps us become more aware of our bodies through movement, my class would switch off.

With the new eyes my treatment had given me, I also began to notice how much effort my students needed to be able to stretch. Stretching should be a release, not a strain. In order to help them become aware of their physical limitations, I had to find a way of encouraging them to relax without realizing it, and also to start enjoying themselves. I needed to create an Eastern exercise class dressed up as an aerobics session from the West.

How to achieve this blend successfully came to me some time later, when I went to visit a physiotherapist for back pain. As I rolled my bottom round on the small ball he had given me to relieve the pain caused by a trapped nerve, the idea struck me. By using the ball to move, stretch and reach, I was stimulating the energy pathways in my body almost effortlessly. As my breathing rate increased, I realized also that my chi (energy) was being stimulated.

A ball, I thought, is the perfect metaphor for energy; it was an object on which my classes could focus their minds; it promoted the kind of awareness, stability and graceful movement that professional Tai Chi and Yoga students take years to achieve. The potential for a fast-track method of feeling the benefits of Eastern exercise in the time it takes to complete an average Western aerobics class was all there, in a ball.

All of this marked the incarnation of the Chi Ball Method. It occurred to me that the philosophy of Eastern medicine provides the perfect frame on which to build a class around the concept of balance.

Intensive study can take years, but through my own healing I came to believe that an understanding of the essence of these Eastern philosophies was enough to induce benefits.

My intention in developing the Chi Ball Method and writing this book is to demystify the principles of some of today's popular ancient and more recent exercise disciplines.

The Chi Ball Method incorporates essences of Tai Chi, Chi Kung, Hatha Yoga, the work of the late Joseph Pilates which I've called Body Conditioning, Feldenkrais and Deep Relaxation, all of which are explained in greater detailed in subsequent chapters.

This book by no means provides an exhaustive explanation of any of the disciplines I describe, but is meant to offer an understanding of why and how they are integrated into the Chi Ball Method. The basis of each discipline has been used to complement the Five Elements energy pattern of Eastern medicine and the concept of balance known as yin and yang. I have endeavoured to bridge the gap between our most popular Western exercise forms and the wisdom of the Eastern ones. A wealth of glorious knowledge and wisdom awaits those of you who finally decide to cross that bridge one day into study of the purist form of Tai Chi, Chi Kung, Yoga, Pilates®, Feldenkrais, Deep Relaxation and Meditation.

Traditional Chinese Medicine also views ill-health as the body challenging and balancing itself. A bone which has been broken is stronger when healed than before. More often than not our immune systems can benefit from a fight to ward off viruses and bacteria. Treat each illness or disharmony as an opportunity to learn and participate in your own health.

So, with the Chi Ball Method I have tried to build a bridge for those wishing to cross over from doing no exercise or more traditional exercise classes to practising routines that go deeper. By taking those elements I believe to be the most effective from Tai Chi, Chi Kung, Yoga, Pilates®, Feldenkrais and Deep Relaxation and adapting them to Western exercise formats with which we are more familiar, I have created a programme that is simple, gentle, rewarding and, I hope, hugely enjoyable. I trust you will be able to use the book as a guide to being balanced, happy and staying well.

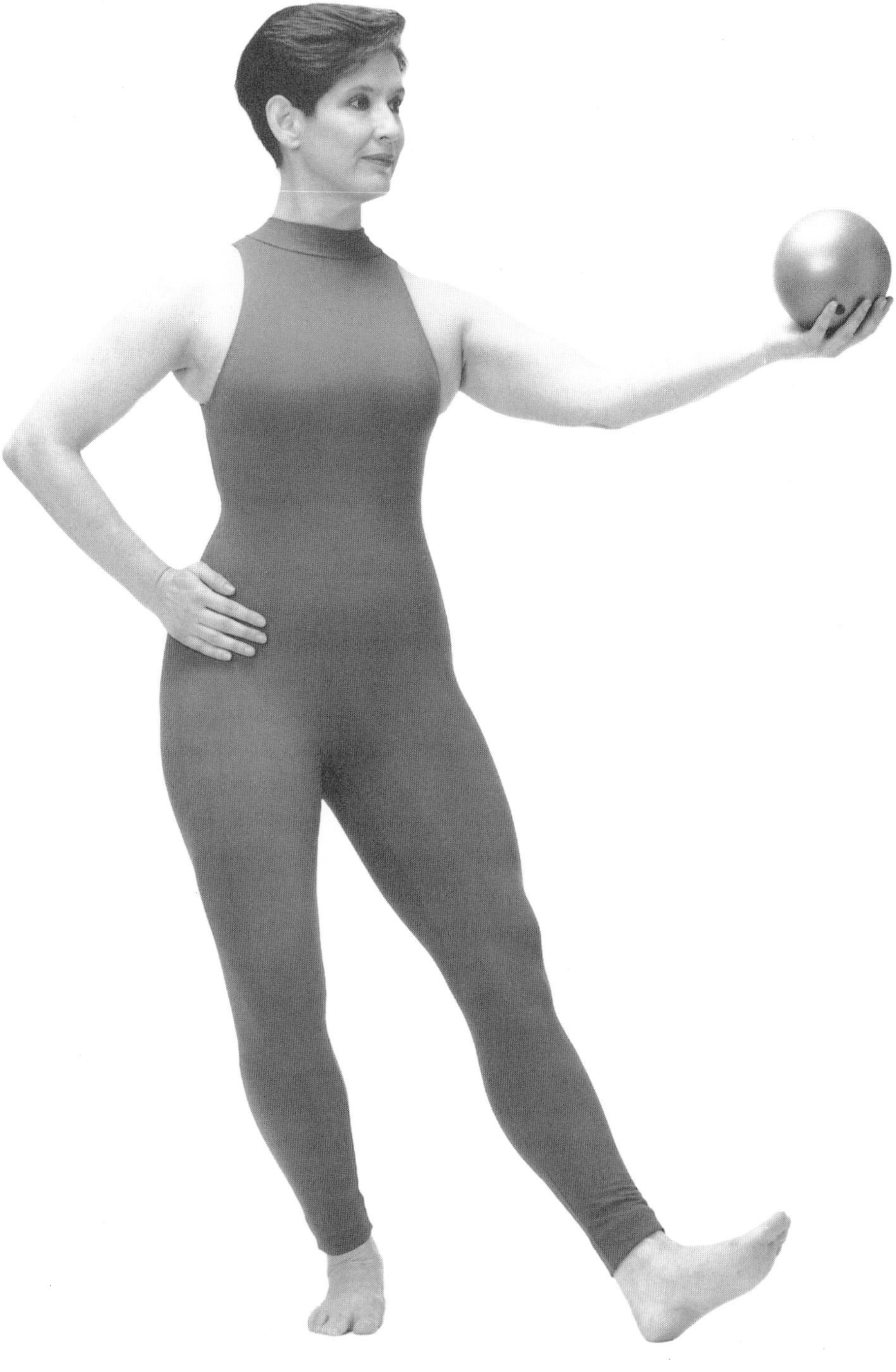

chapter one

the precepts of traditional chinese medicine

Traditional Chinese Medicine (TCM) is based on the philosophy of The *Tao* (pronounced 'dow') meaning 'The Way'. Its practice, Taoism, is between 5,000 and 8,000 years old. Incorporating The Tao into our lives means living and working in harmony with the laws of nature, the rhythms of which affect our energy levels, our physical health and the state of our minds. Stress, depression, sickness and disease, according to the principles of TCM, are all the result of living and working against The Tao.

In order to live in a way which promotes good health, practitioners of TCM help individuals to achieve balance in their body, mind and spirit. In contrast to the conventional Western approach, which treats only that part our physical body showing any sign of illness, TCM considers also our thoughts and emotions and our vitality, as well as our body's need for treatment. All have a significant effect on our well-being.

TCM has as its premise four basic precepts, which are considered when diagnosing an individual's health and attempting to reinstate balance to the mind, body and spirit:

- the theory of yin and yang
- the Five Elements
- the meridian system
- chi, our vital energy.

Yin and Yang

Yang has its root in Yin

Yin has its root in Yang.

Without Yin, Yang cannot arise.

Without Yang, Yin cannot be born.

Yin alone cannot arise; Yang alone cannot grow.

Yin and Yang are divisible but inseparable.

Nei Jing

Most people are familiar with the classic black-and-white symbol that represents yin and yang. The way in which the two opposites are entwined illustrates their working together to achieve balance. They are considered the polarities of life. Neither yang nor yin is ever dominant, as each contains an element of the other, held together by an energetic tension. In spite of being individual entities, they cannot function as such: this is The Tao (nature's Way).

In their striving for balance yin and yang energies are in constant motion, yin being what is still, silent and condensed, while yang is all that is active, expressive and expansive. The same duality exists in our minds, bodies and spirits.

Examples of The Tao – that is, the continuous compromise between yin and yang – can be seen all around us. Take the pattern of the seasons. The yang energy which peaks in Summer has eventually to give way to the yin energy of Autumn. In Winter, ice-cold yin must yield in the Spring to the warm, expansive energy of yang.

There is a similar occurrence in nature's recycling of water (yin), which is evaporated by the heat of the sun and moves up until transformed into vapour (yang). Once cooled, the vapour turns to rain (yin).

While there is a natural balancing of this continuous ebb and flow of energy in all of us, many flout it, becoming either too yin or too yang. Consider our bodies' reaction to the onset of Winter. When it is cold (yang) our blood thickens and our digestion slows, so we have more fat stores as protection from the weather – all indications of a time for hibernation and stillness. What do we do? Panic about any weight gain by ceasing to eat the very foods the body requires in the cold, continue with whatever work or social schedule we have followed at any other time of the year, and subject our bodies to often punishing exercise regimes to atone for the excesses of Christmas or other festive celebrations. Is it any wonder we catch colds and feel drained of energy?

Fighting nature's balancing act results in illness, and often our lifestyle itself is completely at odds with this process. We are generally in the West goal-oriented, achievement-driven and overly active in the wrong ways and at inappropriate times, as a result of which we become impatient, frustrated – bad-tempered, even. Our lives are too yang-focused and many of us would benefit from being more yin, which requires more detachment and being more receptive, observant and accepting.

According to TCM we can experience physical indications of a yin/yang imbalance in our body, mind or spirit up to six months before it manifests as sickness or injury. TCM attempts, where necessary, to help restore the natural balance and so avoid any sort of ill-health.

Yin and Yang in Health

As mentioned earlier, when we flout the laws of nature we become unwell. Depending on how far along the yin or yang scale we stray, nature will attempt to enforce balance.

YANG

driving personality, constant travelling, constant exposure
to stressfull environments/situations, emotionally holding on tight,
virtually no rest, irratic eating patterns.

highly stressed, excessively overworking, too much alchohol,
excessive emotional expression: anger, rage, fear, worry

little rest, little sleep, poor diet, overworking

8 hrs working/30 mins exercise, 30 mins relaxation per day

BALANCE

stable emotions, strong immune system, balanced health

colds, flu, allergies, viruses, constant headaches, general lethargy

prone to accidents or injuries: back pain, sprained ankle, shoulders etc.
minor health scares: high blood pressure, anxiety attacks, poor digestion

glandular fever, chronic fatigue syndrome, depression, personal crisis
serious health scare: surgery

YIN

The Yin/Yang Polarity Scale of Health

Winter is a time of rest and recuperation. There is more dark than light, the atmospheric temperature is greatly reduced. It is also, it seems, a time of increased incidence of colds, flu or allergies. In the past our ancestors would go to bed as soon as it was dark and rise with the light. Our body's energy naturally responds to light or darkness and responds badly to the dictates of our modern timetable.

Our Western obsession with dieting further attacks and depletes the body. According to TCM, in Winter it is essential to carry more weight and to eat warming foods. TCM's approach to nutrition is very simple. In Summer, eat foods grown above ground or raw, with very little red meat. In Winter, eat foods grown below the ground or well cooked, including some red meat. These more dense and warming yang-type foods counteract the Condensed Yin of Winter.

If we overexpress the yang energy in Winter, we will suffer ill-health. Colds, flus and viruses are nature's way of intervening to try to force us to slow down.

Living, working and exercising in harmony with the yin/yang cycle helps us to create balance in our bodies and minds, and therefore stay truly well.

Understanding the Cycle of Yin and Yang

The Tao teaches us that all life is cyclical. This cycle of energy is beautifully expressed in nature's seasons.

There are five expressions of the yin/yang energy in the seasons.

In Spring we have Rising Yang, a time when the daffodils and tulips push up through the soil, buds appear on trees and the sun begins rising earlier.

As the energy pushes towards Summer, it is called Radiant Yang. The trees and flowers bloom in abundance and everything seems to shine.

Summer declines into Late Summer, and is called Descending Yang. This is a time of harvest, when the energy and light of day steadily fall.

With the arrival of Autumn we have Rising Yin, as nature winds down in preparation for the Winter by ridding itself of unnecessary foliage and becoming more calm and quiet.

Finally we have the complete stillness of Winter, known as Condensed Yin. Nature is in hibernation, still, reflective and quiet. From this place of quiet, great energy is made.

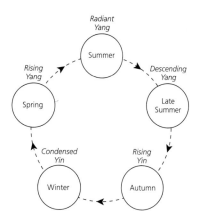

The Yin/Yang Seasonal Energy Cycle

Observing the philosophy of the yin/yang cycle of energy will bring profound balance and well-being into your life. Using our own personal experience of feeling healthy, strong and energetic is a natural reference point. When our health deviates from this centre, an awareness of the yin/yang cycle can help us to maintain and conserve our vital energy and prevent ill-health, chronic fatigue or disease. The yin/yang philosophy helps us to participate in our own healing.

This cycle can also be applied to the course of a week or a day.

The 24-Hour Yin/Yang Cycle

Dawn to mid-morning is considered to be Rising Yang. This is an ideal time to meditate, exercise or engage in intense mental work. Disciplining ourselves to rise an hour earlier to exercise at dawn will improve our energy levels and ability to concentrate throughout the day.

Mid-morning to mid-afternoon is Radiant Yang. This, the warmest part of the day, is when we are usually at our most hospitable and is a good time for meetings, discussions, debates and job interviews. It is also a good time for exercise.

Mid- to late afternoon is Descending Yang. This is often a time when some of us feel a little lethargic. A short break to take a walk or do some breathing exercises lifts the body's energy.

Late afternoon to late evening is Rising Yin. The body is winding down in preparation for sleep. This is not an ideal time for excessive exercise – a difficult regime to adhere to in our

Western society, where the working day ends between 5 p.m. and 6 p.m. and our social activities begin.

Late evening to dawn is Condensed Yin. Deep sleep and stillness give the body and mind an opportunity to rejuvenate and rebalance. If a night's sleep is deep and replenishing, the Rising Yang energy is strong and forceful, making early-morning exercise vigorous and effortless.

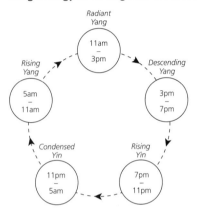

The Yin/Yang 24-Hour Energy Cycle

The Weekly Yin/Yang Cycle

Once again we start the cycle with Rising Yang, on Monday. Mondays are ideal for gentle to mildly energetic exercise routines.

Tuesday/Wednesday can be seen as Radiant Yang, when energy is at its highest level. Exercise routines that create heat and promote strength and flexibility – such as aerobics – bring the body to an energetic peak.

Thursday is Descending Yang. Exercise should be less strenuous – this is in any case a day on which we often start contemplating the weekend. It is interesting to note that Thursday-evening fitness classes will often have a significantly lower attendance than those held earlier in the week.

Friday/Saturday is Rising Yin. Our energy is at its lowest. Stretch-based exercise, such as Yoga, Tai Chi, Body Conditioning mat-work class or Feldenkrais, is a good option.

Sunday is Condensed Yin. The tradition of no work on Sundays complements the yin/yang philosophy of Sunday being a time for stillness, reflection and rest.

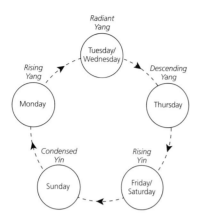

Radiant Yang — Tuesday/Wednesday

Rising Yang — Monday

Descending Yang — Thursday

Condensed Yin — Sunday

Rising Yin — Friday/Saturday

The Yin/Yang Weekly Energy Cycle

The Chi Ball Method Yin/Yang Cycle

Incorporating the philosophy of yin and yang in the Chi Ball Method makes it a new and unique approach to exercise. Once we feel the full effect of the five aspects of the yin/yang energy within us, we become more in tune with how we move and express our physical, mental and emotional energy from day to day, week to week, or throughout the seasons.

A typical Chi Ball class will awaken the body with Tai Chi–Chi Kung. This stimulates the breathing and raises the energy of the body – Rising Yang.

This is followed by a series of energetic and vigorous movements, co-ordinated with rhythmic breathing, to stimulate the cardiovascular system and stretch and tone the meridian system. Yoga Standing postures correspond with the Radiant Yang energy.

Exercises based on techniques taught by Joseph Pilates use the breath and emphasize core inner strength and stability, which embody Descending Yang. Seated Yoga postures can also be incorporated at this stage of the class.

Feldenkrais Method promotes effortless repetitive movement patterns, to help us change long-term habits which are causing tension, discomfort or even pain. This pleasurable and immensely relaxing part of the class corresponds to the Rising Yin energy.

Finally, at least 10 minutes of Deep Relaxation and 10 to 20 minutes of Meditation allow us to feel and practise Condensed Yin.

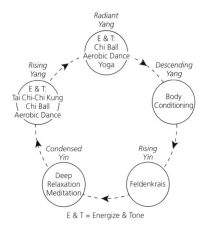

The Yin/Yang Chi Ball Energy Cycle

Tao is Mother of the Whole

The Whole splits into Yin and Yang

From these two comes three;

from three comes all life.

Yin is form, the container.

Yang is essence, the contained

Like the in-breath and the out-breath of Life,

these two are one.

Lao Tzu's *Tao te Ching*

The Five Elements

Yin and yang is the root and trunk of all creation;

the Five Elements are the branches that bear leaves,

flowers and fruits of the universe.

Mantak Chia, *Inner Structure of Tai Chi*

With this part of TCM theory we start to build a picture of the correlation between our health and that of the natural world. If any more evidence were needed that our own health is inherently tied up with that of the planet on which we live, we should consider the following quote from the 2nd-century BC Chinese philosopher, Master Huai Nan …

The heavens have four seasons, five elements, nine divisions and 366 days.

Man has four limbs, five viscera, nine orifices and 366 sections.

Heaven has wind, rain, cold and heat.

Man too has a 'taking in' and a 'giving out'; joy and anger.

Thus the gall corresponds to the clouds;

the lungs are vapour breath;

the liver is wind;

the kidneys are rain;

and the spleen is thunder.

Catastrophes and chaos in our world are as much a cause of an imbalance in nature as is sickness in a human being, the practitioners of Traditional Chinese Medicine believe. Moreover, if we took greater care of ourselves, our collective respect for the planet would be naturally enhanced. Modern scientists say we have just 20 years before damage to the planet becomes irreversible. Could the same be true of the human race?

Wood, fire, earth, metal and water are the five natural elements through which yin and yang energies are expressed. Each is associated with an internal organ and a season of the year, as illustrated in the table opposite. When trying to diagnose the causes of illness in a patient, TCM practitioners will consider the body's natural cycle, the balance of yin and yang, and the influence of any of the Five Elements on the individual's health. TCM aligns the inner organ with each of the elements and its corresponding cycle. When a breakdown in health occurs, the practitioner will begin forming a picture of how the disharmony occurred by referring to the Five Elements theory.

Element	Colour	Season	Corresponding Organs	Yin/Yang Phase
Wood	Green	Spring	Liver/Gallbladder	Rising Yang
Fire	Red	Summer	Heart/Small Intestine	Radiant Yang
Earth	Yellow	Late Summer	Stomach/Spleen	Descending Yang
Metal	Silver/White	Autumn	Lungs/Large Intestine	Rising Yin
Water	Dark Blue/ Black	Winter	Kidneys/Bladder	Condensed Yin

The Five Elements could be said to represent five phases, as in nature. As with yin and yang we see a cyclical pattern, with each element being able to contribute and, at the same time, yield to the others. These processes are known as the creating cycle and the controlling cycle.

The Creating Cycle

In the creating cycle one element feeds off and contributes to another in the natural course of the circular flow. Water feeds wood, which can be burned by fire into ashes, which feed the earth minerals and metals, which are components of water.

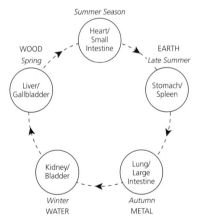

The Creating Energy Cycle

As can be seen, the pattern is repeated with our organs: the Wood Element organs (the liver and gallbladder) help to store and supply the Fire Element organs (heart and small intestine). These Fire Element organs carry oxygenated blood and metabolic energy to the Earth Element organs (stomach and spleen). The stomach and spleen provide nourishment to the Metal Element organs (the lungs and large intestine) and to the Water Element organs (kidneys and bladder). Finally, the kidneys generate blood for the liver, and so the cycle continues.

The Controlling Cycle

In the controlling cycle all elements inter-react, with each affecting or being affected by the others.

Water will restrain fire; wood grows in and covers the earth, preventing its depletion and erosion by wind or water; fire restrains metal by making it soft and malleable; earth controls water by creating banks for rivers and basins for lakes; metal stops wood from overgrowing, as when metal tools are used to cut woody plants and trees down.

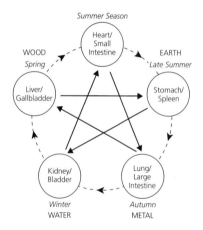

The Controlling Energy Cycle

In terms of our health, the controlling cycle sees the Wood Element organs (the liver and gallbladder) supply energy to the Earth Element organs (the stomach and spleen), which are responsible for transforming and transporting food, and controlling the moisture of the Water

Element organs (the kidneys and bladder), which are responsible for the conservation of our essential life-energy *jing* and fluid control. The kidneys and bladder will then keep the Fire Element organs (the heart and small intestine) cool and moist. These Fire Element organs (the heart, governor of the blood, and small intestine, receiver and converter of food) control the Metal Element organs (the lungs, which govern breathing and chi distribution, and the large intestine).

TCM teaches us that the inner organs are working partnerships. Each pair of inner organs is also aligned with the seasons, so as we follow nature's example of rising and falling energy our health becomes balanced and harmonious.

When a pair of organs (or one organ within the partnership) is dysfunctional, the next pair of organs in the controlling or creating cycle will be affected. For example, if the kidney energy is strong, the kidneys will be effective in cooling and in restraining excessive heat in the heart. A grey pallor or redness in the face, high or low blood pressure, angina and insomnia, on the other hand, are possible indications that either the liver and gallbladder (creating cycle) or the kidneys (controlling cycle) are too weak to lend their support to the heart.

Our emotions also affect the health of the inner organs. The heart is said to house the *shen*, or spirit. Some Chinese texts call the heart 'the dwelling place of the mind'. Emotional signs of heart disharmony are severe agitation, restlessness, absent-mindedness, erratic thinking, cold-heartedness, overenthusiasm followed by deep disillusionment, constant nervous laughter or chatter, and a lack of a sense of humour.

Each element is also associated with a time of year:

Winter, a time of hibernation, reflection and stillness, is represented by water.
The new growth and flowering of Spring are associated with wood.
Fire represents the vibrancy and high passion of Summer.
The harvest and gathering-in of Late Summer are reflected in the characteristics of earth.
The density and consolidation of Autumn are reflected in the characteristics of metal.

As we try to align the energy within ourselves with that of the natural world, the pattern of the seasons gives us a perfect indication of how and when we should alter our behaviour, and this applies as much to the exercise we take as to any other aspect of our lives.

The Five Elements in Exercise

The energy cycle of the seasons mirrors that of yin and yang. In Spring the energy rises, peaking in the Summer. Energy is consolidated during Late Summer and begins to wane as Autumn comes. During Winter, energy comes to a standstill.

Element	Season	Nature's Response	*In Energy Terms*	Chi Ball Elements
Wood	Spring	new growth	*rising energy*	Energize & Tone: *Tai Chi–Chi Kung, Chi Ball Aerobic Dance*
Fire	Summer	full bloom	*high/peak energy*	Energize & Tone: *Chi Ball Aerobic Dance*, Yoga
Earth	Late Summer	harvesting time	*consolidating, compounding energy*	Body Conditioning
Metal	Autumn	reducing	*waning energy*	Feldenkrais
Water	Winter	hibernation	*slow, silent energy*	Deep Relaxation

We have now reached a point of understanding the basis upon which Chi Ball is built. Exercise is not done, therefore, under obligation to lose weight, because of general health concerns or to keep in step with fashion. Now we have a personal reason and purpose behind our intention to participate in regular exercise. It is far more interesting and meaningful to observe the natural world around us and plan our exercise regimes accordingly.

Chi Ball Method uses five exercise disciplines to reflect the seasonal energies as expressed in the Five Element theory: Tai Chi–Chi Kung, Yoga, Body Conditioning, Feldenkrais and Deep Relaxation. Using each of these disciplines will be discussed in Chapter 3.

Having familiarized ourselves with TCM's philosophy of balance and seasonal energy, we can now increase our awareness and depth of knowledge to include the meridian system.

The Meridian System

The meridians move the chi and blood, regulate yin and yang, moisten tendons and bones, benefiting the joints.

Nei Jing

Just as our veins are the channels through which our blood flows, the body's network of meridians acts as the irrigation system of our chi (energy). The meridians run down each side of the body, rather like a system of electrical wiring, and the points at which they can be stimulated could be thought of as light bulbs.

There are said to be more than 50 meridians in the body, although it is more common today to work with just 14. Ten of these have a direct association with our main internal organs, while the other four are responsible for the regulation of our body temperature, the flow of fluids from one organ to another and for supporting the entire meridian network. If at any time the flow through this network is blocked, cells, tissues, ligaments, muscles and our organs can suffer as our chi is prevented from reaching certain parts of the body.

The organs, which work in partnerships and are governed by the 10 main meridians are:

- the liver and gallbladder
- the heart and small intestine
- the stomach and spleen
- the lungs and large intestine
- and the kidneys and bladder.

The meridians of the Pericardium and Triple Heater protect the heart and control the flow of blood and nutrients. The Pericardium is the outer membrane surrounding the heart, which protects the organ from emotional stresses and strains. The Triple Heater governs the body's energy pathways, so keeping the body nourished and the circulation in good order.

The 13th and 14th meridians are called the Governing and Conception Vessels. Both act as the junctions through which all other meridians pass, regulating and ensuring the flow of chi and the balance of yin and yang energies. These last two have strong influences over our central nervous system, state of mind, ability to conceive (pregnancy) and spiritual awareness.

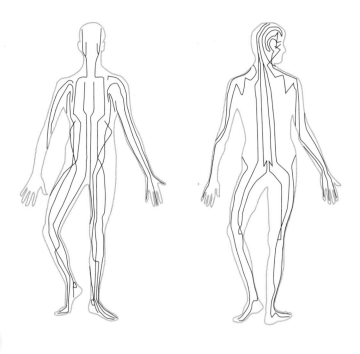

The Meridian System

Lethargy, poor circulation, headaches, back pain and muscular tension can all be symptoms of a blocked or imbalanced meridian, which occurs when there is either too little or too much chi. In Traditional Chinese Medicine this is referred to as depleted or stagnant chi, which becomes either weak or lodged in a particular meridian. Stagnant chi must be released to revitalize the body and ease associated aches and pains. This is done by stimulating certain points along the meridians, the same points that are commonly used in acupuncture, acupressure and exercises such as Tai Chi, Chi Kung and Yoga, to enable chi to flow freely again.

Certain physical manifestations are indications of an imbalance or blockage in a particular meridian:

Organs and Meridians	Physical Signs of Imbalance
Liver/Gallbladder	Eye problems, stiff tense muscles, tight ligaments and tendons, poor muscle tone, brittle or weak nails, migraines, nausea, impaired vision, ear problems, tension in neck and shoulders, abscesses, lethargy
Heart/Small intestine (Pericardium/Triple Heater)	Red/flushed complexion, irregular heart beat, little or excessive perspiration, low or high blood pressure, speech problems (stuttering), insomnia, hyperactive, painful dry eczema
Spleen/Stomach	Distended abdomen, prolapse of inner organs, bruises easily, weight problems, sluggish energy, rough, dry skin, poor digestion, chronic sweet tooth, poor muscle tone
Lungs/Large intestine	Sinus headaches, nasal congestion, throat problems, constipation, eczema, psoriasis, breathing problems, poor circulation, melancholy or depressed
Kidneys/Bladder	Sciatica, constant thirst, bladder infections, chronic fatigue, dark circles under the eyes, poor or frequent urination, osteoporosis, infertility and impotence, poor stamina, eye problems, ear infections, backache, skeletal problems, premature greying

How Emotions Play a Part in Our Internal Health

Each of the meridians discussed so far is also associated with a particular emotion, and too little or too much of any one can affect the health of the organ with which it is linked. Impatience and frustration, for example, can damage the liver; fear and fright affect the kidneys; our gallbladder responds adversely to anger and rage; and the lungs are susceptible to grief. Worry upsets the spleen, while overly exuberant joy or hysteria takes its toll on the heart. All of these can result in a chi blockage, as though the energy becomes lodged or stuck, this can lead, like a blood clot, to sickness or disease.

The Meridians	Corresponding Emotions
Lungs/Large intestine	**Grief**: inability to 'let go' of disappointment, pessimism, narrow-mindedness
Spleen/Stomach	**Worry**: obsession, poor concentration, scattered mind, feeling of being 'stuck' in life, insecurity, craving for sympathy, emotional worries
Kidneys/Bladder	**Fear**: depression, unpredictability, feeling of being unable to 'cope', panic attacks, fear of failure, apprehension
Heart/Small intestine, Heart Constrictor (Pericardium) and Triple Heater	**Joy**: hysteria, excessive laughter, lack of warmth, being overly critical, cynicism, naivety, overthinking and working, feelings of vulnerability, feeling unsafe and unprotected in life, inability to relax, defensiveness, cautiousness, oversensitivity
Liver/Gallbladder	**Anger**: frustration, impatience, irritability, resentfulness, long-term rage, jealousy, aggression

The role of each organ partnership is threefold: they keep us alive, drive our motivations for being alive, and enable us to feel what it is to be alive. Therefore, the balance of these three roles must be maintained if we are to achieve good health in the truest sense.

Partner Meridians and Organs	Life Functions	Root Emotion	Psychological Functions	Highest Expression
Liver and gallbladder	Evolution and adaptation – movement and growth	Anger	Purpose – foresight – adaptability	Compassion
Heart and small intestine/Pericardium /Triple Heater	Self-realization – idealization and fulfilment	Joy	Awareness – self-identity – harmony – love	Love
Spleen/Pancreas and stomach	Concretization – nourishment	Worry	Concentration – cognition – sympathy	Empathy
Lungs and large intestine	Transmutation and synthesis interchange	Grief	Boundary – instinct – interaction	Reverence
Kidneys and bladder	Procreation survival	Fear	Will-power – stamina – ingenuity	Wisdom

Chi Ball and the Meridians

The meridians, like most other parts of our anatomy, can be preserved and taken care of by doing regular exercise. The movement, deeper breathing and heat generated by certain types of exercise are believed to help cleanse and revitalize the meridian channels, thereby enhancing the flow of chi to our organs.

To achieve this the Chi Ball Method uses the principles of Tai Chi, Chi Kung and Yoga in dance-like sequences, which vary in pace from being slow and gentle (yin) to being energetic and fast (yang). The focused breathing and repetitive, fluid moves aid the release of muscular and emotional tension and dislodge blockages to the flow of our chi.

We should finish this part of a Chi Ball session, in which the ball is used to help us concentrate and be aware of where our meridians lie, with better circulation, greater flexibility, enhanced lung capacity, loss of tension and stiffness and improved concentration, co-ordination and balance.

Chi – The Vital Energy

Tao produced the One
The one produced the two
The two produced the three
And the three produced the ten thousand things.
The ten thousand things carry the Yin and embrace the Yang
and through the blending of the Chi they achieve perfect harmony.

Lao Tzu, *Tao te Ching*

The Chinese call it *chi*, the Japanese *ki* and in India it is known as *prana*. The closest Western translation is 'vital energy' or 'basic life-force', which according to ancient Eastern philosophies is present in all life. When this energy flows freely, the mind, body and spirit are alert and work harmoniously; when blocked, their function is inhibited and ill-health can result.

There are seven types of chi. Learning about these seven types gives us an understanding of how the health of the physical, mental and emotional body is acquired, sustained, depleted and then healed:

1   breath chi
2   food chi
3   original chi
4   internal chi
5   external chi
6   nutritive chi
7   protective chi.

We will now look at each type of chi in turn.

Breath Chi

As important to our health as the quantity and quality of the air we breathe is the way in which it is inhaled and expelled. Poor breathing affects the functioning of our brain, including our memory and concentration levels, our emotional stability, heart, lungs, muscles, circulation and our nervous system. Because oxygen is believed to be the engine of our chi (energy), deep breathing from the diaphragm (known as diaphragmatic breathing) is necessary when the flow of chi through the body needs re-stimulating.

Food Chi

Food is another vital source of our life-force. The Chinese have an ancient cultural tradition of taking great care to plan and prepare their meals in ways that preserve it. Vegetables are always cut in a certain way (to mimic the direction in which chi naturally flows), and all cooking is over a flame; electricity and especially microwaving destroys the chi of food. Yang foods, such as vegetables that grow below ground, dairy produce, fish and red meat, are eaten in Winter, while in Summer lettuce, tomatoes, cucumbers and other overground-grown vegetables, plus soya produce, light fish and white meat – all yin food – are consumed.

Original Chi

The chi with which we are born is known as original chi and comprises what is known as our 'constitution'. To some extent the quality of our original chi is predetermined by the health of our parents at the time of our conception. How old they were, the quality of their diet, and their general state of health mentally, physically and emotionally, all affect our inherited chi.

Those born with a strong constitution (high-quality, high levels of chi) often take their natural good health for granted and go through life abusing it, until it is weakened to the extent that they become ill. Weak chi at birth, on the other hand, will require constant effort, by way of correct nutrition, moderate exercise, proper breathing and a sense of contentment, to sustain and strengthen the constitution and thereby avoid sickness.

Internal Chi

This is the chi upon which our internal body relies for its health and proper function. Internal chi flows with the blood to all our inner organs and through all the meridians, helping to keep yin and yang energies shifting and our body in balance. Too much physical activity can erode internal chi, whereas complete inactivity will cause it to stagnate. Moderate amounts of sufficiently energetic daily movement and exercise, however, are essential for the necessary stimulation and free flow of our internal chi.

External Chi

This type of energy is around and surrounds us, but can be sensed and effectively accessed only by the very sensitive. Highly trained Chi Kung masters, for example, can read our spiritual or subtle bodies for signs of physical imbalance or disease. Along with acupuncture, acupressure and reiki, Chi Kung can be used to heal, recharge and rebalance an unwell organ that has been revealed in our external chi.

Nutritive Chi

Nutritive chi moves with the blood via the heart and blood vessels to deliver and ensure nourishment to our inner organs, cells, tissues, muscles and bones.

Protective Chi

Moisture from the pores of the skin and sweat glands form a protective layer of chi between the skin and muscles, which when strongly fortified form a barrier against invading germs, viruses and chills. This protective chi helps the body resist, fight and expel infections that manage to penetrate the natural lines of defence.

There are two other chi types worth mentioning: stagnant chi and rebellious chi.

Stagnant Chi

Muscular aches and pains and malfunctioning organs are often caused by stagnant chi. Coughing is a sign of chi lodged in the lungs; abdominal bloating can be indicative of stagnant chi in the liver.

Rebellious Chi

This is stagnant chi that has started to move in the wrong direction. Nausea, vomiting, burping, heartburn and hiccoughs are manifestations of the presence of rebellious chi.

Chi and the 24-Hour Body Clock

Being aware of how we feel at particular times of the day is one way of coming to understand how the energy flow through our organs contributes to our mental and physical well-being. The concentration of chi and blood flow through our organs changes approximately every two hours, which is why we experience energy highs and lows. By midnight, chi is at its most yin (quiet, slow, still), retreating deep into the body, whereas at midday it is at full yang (expressive, bountiful), which is when we should feel most alert and energetic. As one organ and its associated meridian fill with chi (become most yang), other organs will be emptying of chi (becoming most yin).

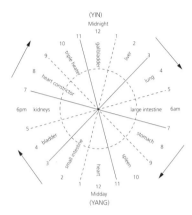

Chi and the 24-Hour Body Clock

As is illustrated in the diagram above, the gallbladder and liver have the highest chi concentration between 11 p.m. and 3 a.m., when the heart and small intestine have the lowest. The liver most efficiently rejuvenates itself when the body is horizontal and at rest. Shift workers, according to these principles, may well experience trouble with the gallbladder, liver and other organs later in life, as these organs will not have had sufficient restful recuperation time.

Between 5 a.m. and 7 a.m., when the large intestine is enjoying the greatest quantity of chi, is the best time to empty the bowels. By 7 a.m., chi is moving on to the stomach and spleen in preparation for the day's first meal. The gradual decrease of chi in the stomach from 9 a.m. onwards also explains why, according to both Chinese and Western medical practitioners, our meals should get lighter as the day progresses. There is more sense than most of us would imagine in the old saying, 'Eat like a king for breakfast, like a prince for lunch and like a pauper for supper.'

The kidneys are considered to be among the most vital but vulnerable of our organs, as they are receiving most chi at a time when, in an effort to keep going during a typical working day, we habitually drain the system of energy. This pattern is self-perpetuating, because the weaker our kidneys become, the more difficult it is for us to concentrate and sustain energy.

Chi and Exercise

Our body relies upon the correct amount and the unburdened flow of chi. Using simple exercises based on movements in Tai Chi, Chi Kung, aerobic dance and Yoga, the Chi Ball Method aims to regulate the balance. Correct breathing, combined with specific exercises, releases any stagnant chi and helps to nourish the meridians and protect our inner organs. An awareness of the 24-hour body clock and the yin/yang energy cycle is our compass, letting us know when best to exercise and when best to rest.

chapter two

the ancient and modern roots of chi ball

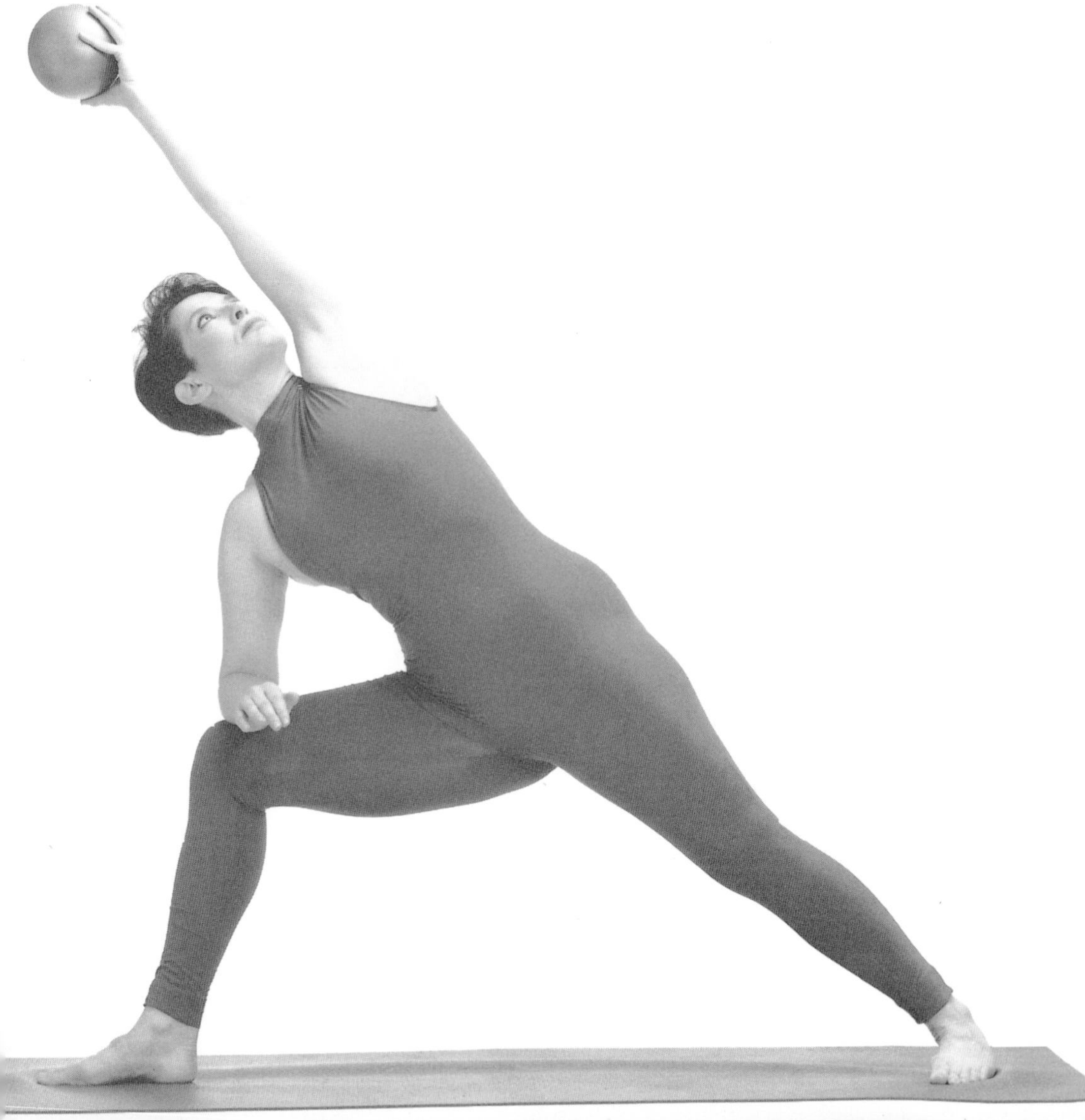

To suit particular seasons of the year, and in concordance with the Five Elements theory, the Chi Ball Method incorporates five exercise disciplines:

1   Energize and Tone (Tai Chi, Chi Kung and Chi Ball Aerobic Dance) for energy, internal health and balance
2   Yoga for strength, flexibility and balance
3   Body Conditioning to stabilize the torso and body control
4   Feldenkrais Method for relaxation and effortless movement
5   Deep Relaxation for harmony, good health and general well-being.

Energize and Tone

Energize and Tone combines Tai Chi, Chi Kung and energetic modern aerobic dance sequences called Chi Ball Aerobic Dance – which uses rhythmic breathing to stir and drive chi through the meridian channels and move the yin and yang energies.

Tai Chi brings flow and relaxation within movement; Chi Kung prepares the breath and internal chi; the Chi Ball Aerobic Dance sequences build heat, which vigorously stimulates the breathing, chi and circulation. As the diaphragm is exercised and stretched, the breathing reverts back to a more natural state. The major meridian channels open as the chi energy begins to flow freely, balancing the yin and yang energies.

Energize and Tone was developed to help many of those who had tried Eastern exercise disciplines but were put off by their inability to do any of the moves. It is in many ways the equivalent of what in the West we call a warm-up, so by the time we move on to the more strenuous aspects of Yoga, the heart rate is up and the body is warm and supple enough to cope.

Tai Chi

Ultimately in tai chi, the aim is to be familiar
with all the different aspects of yourself;
when they are unified, you are integrated.

Paul Brecher, *Principles of Tai Chi*

Tai Chi, best described as a soft martial art and originally practised as a form of self-defence, is based on the philosophy of The Tao (or The Way, as mentioned in Chapter 1). It is variously described today as 'supreme ultimate' or the 'way of supreme harmony', names which reflect the yin/yang aspects of the moves and techniques. We sink down and rise up; retreat back then move forward; bend down and straighten up, all the time using gentleness with control as we focus simultaneously on the inside and outside of our bodies.

While providing a physical and mental challenge, Tai Chi is also considered to be one of the most therapeutic forms of exercise. Through Tai Chi we permit the free flow of chi and true balance. When flowing unimpeded throughout the meridian network, chi fortifies our immune system, allowing renewed energy into areas of stagnation. This relieves aches, pains and stiffness as our tendons, muscles, bones and nervous system are nourished and the health of our organs is maintained.

As Tai Chi also works on an emotional level, our stagnant attitudes or narrow-mindedness, which might have impeded our health and mental progress, can also be made to change. Free-flowing chi makes for a healthy body, mind and spirit.

In line with the principles of yin and yang, balance can only be reached by practising opposites: detachment in times of stress, and forgiveness in times of strife. Equally, true strength is achieved only when we are familiar with complete stillness and relaxation. Learning this can take time, but as we become stronger internally through practising Tai Chi, we acquire an exterior that reflects this inner strength.

Breathing

Many beginners experience difficulty with the slow and gentle breathing used in Tai Chi, which demands use of the entire diaphragm. Through long-term stress, emotional worries, an inability to relax and extremely poor posture, most adults have forgotten how to breathe and instead inhale and exhale in shallow gasps, using only the upper chest. Re-learning a more natural breathing pattern can in and of itself have a profoundly beneficial effect on our health.

How to Breathe

Correct breathing should come from the *dan tien* (navel centre). To see how this feels, place your hands just beneath your navel with the fingertips touching (see page **167**). Now, breathe in through the nose and feel the hands move apart as the abdomen swells, then breathe out through the mouth. As the abdomen shrinks, the hands should meet again. (To avoid hyperventilation, which is common when first practising breathing exercises, breathe out for longer than you breathe in.) Eventually you should be able to breathe both in and out through the nose.

How to Practise Tai Chi

To be at its most effective, Tai Chi demands that we concentrate on five specific aspects of our body:

The Internal Body	Become familiar with where your organs are and which meridians run through them. As you move and breathe, imagine chi flowing through your organs along the meridians.
The External Body	Become aware of how you feel on the outside; can you feel your skin and hair, or how your shoes or clothes cover parts of your body? Think about the way you are standing and the sensation when walking or moving your arms and legs.
Awareness of the Front	Now concentrate on the front of your body, feeling it stretch as you breathe in. When moving forward (yang), focus once more on your front.
Awareness of the Back	As you breathe out, you should feel a relaxing, gently descending sensation in your back. Concentrate on this part of your body when doing any backward (yin) movements.
Central Awareness	Bring your attention to the dan tien (navel centre) of your body. Feel its power as you breathe in. Breathe out and extend down the arms, legs and up your spine.

It is with this awareness that you can move on to a deeper focus on your posture, stability and balance. This is achieved by learning how to control the torso, limbs, head, and eventually the movement of chi.

Basic Stance

1   Without shoes and feeling the whole of each foot flat against the floor, place your feet shoulder-width apart.

2   To help centre yourself, imagine roots growing out of the soles of your feet into the ground.

3   To prevent chi becoming blocked or the circulation from being impeded, softly bend the knees, allowing the weight of your body to sink down.

4   Brace your shoulders slightly and stretch up with the head so the spine is slowly straightened, and allow your tail bone to move in a little. Try now to feel the extra space in your central body and see if you can sense any stiffness or tension. Gradually sink down, keeping your spine straight.

5   Relax your shoulders, arms, hands and your breathing.

6   Your fingers should feel light and the centre of your palms warm.

7   Although in a soft stance, your legs will feel powerful. Spread your feet and toes out to make as much contact as is possible with the ground.

8   To ensure that you are at your most stable, bend the knees a little more, ensuring your weight is over the heels of your feet. Push your knees outwards a little towards the smallest toe, creating a slight twist in your lower leg. You should now feel a firm foundation with the ground.

Posture

1   Your spine should be straight and your tail bone tucked in.

2   Shoulders must be directly over your pelvis or dan tien (navel centre).

3   The weight of your body should be such that your pelvis is now positioned between the heel and centre of your foot.

4   Move from the waist, or dan tien, and let the rest of the upper body follow a split second later. Using the waist first, followed closely by the upper body, keep the body moving as a whole and complete unit.

5   So long as your back is straight, chi can travel along the spine with ease – chi becomes stuck when the shoulders are collapsed and the spine is rounded.

6   Throughout these moves, be aware of the position of your head. Keep it up by pulling it back a little and making sure the ears sit directly above the shoulders. Try to notice if one side of your neck feels any different from the other, and feel the movement in the neck vertebrae front and back.

7   Always allow the fingers to be light and feel the warmth in your palms. Keep your arms relaxed.

Drawing and Directing Chi

You can become aware of, and learn to guide, the flow of chi as the body draws it into the dan tien through the soles of your feet, the palms of your hands and the crown of your head.

Feeling Chi

By focusing on key areas of your body you can actually feel the body becoming charged with chi. The following are signs of the presence of chi:

- warm hands, feet and face
- tingling fingers
- general body warmth, which could be an indication that the core temperature of the body has risen. This means chi is circulating throughout the body.

Earthing and Moving the Body

1   When transferring weight from one leg to the other, keep a 60/40 pressure ratio.

2   As you lean across from one foot to the other, make sure that the weight-bearing leg carries 60 per cent of the body's weight while the other leg retains 40 per cent.

3   Your legs should be working hard but without effort and you should remain centred.

4   Focus once more on your dan tien and be aware of your body as an entire unit or centre of energy.

5   Remain as relaxed as you can during these movements, keeping your mind from wandering by concentrating all the time on your body.

Relaxing and Moving the Body

1   Imagine as you practise each move that you are in a pool of water. Let the arms and legs float and move slowly without effort while remaining completely relaxed.

2   Co-ordinate your breathing with the moves: Inhale as you turn and exhale as you extend a limb; inhale as you prepare to move and exhale as you transfer your weight from one leg to the other.

There are five basic movement patterns within Tai Chi exercise:

Up and down	Movements which involve an ascent and descent
Forward and back	Moving the body forward from one foot to the other and then moving back again, or travelling backward and forward
Sideways	Moving or travelling laterally
Away from the axis	Arm and leg movements which extend outwards and away from the centre of the body
Towards the axis	Arm and leg movements which pull inward or move towards the centre of the body.

Tai Chi and Chi Ball

In the Chi Ball Method we use the basic principles of Tai Chi to learn relaxation through movement and how to assume a stable and solid stance. Through practice we can become strong yet flexible and move in a controlled but graceful manner. By focusing on how we feel inside while moving, we come to know the feeling of balance.

Chi Kung

Chi kung therapy, as well as other branches of Chinese medicine, can be reduced to two simple principles: the cleansing of meridians to achieve harmonious energy flow, and the restoration of yin–yang balance.

Wong Kiew Kit, *The Art of Chi Kung*

Roughly translated, Chi Kung (also spelled Qi Gong) means 'the art of cultivating chi'. While Tai Chi can be practised to prevent illness, Chi Kung is done to cure it and to restore balance and health to mind, body and spirit. Its practice has been known to help sufferers overcome many serious illnesses such as cancer, heart disease, asthma, arthritis, Chronic Fatigue Syndrome and everyday ailments like stomach bugs, digestive problems and other niggling aches and pains.

As has been discussed in other parts of the book, illness or disharmony in the body occurs when the balance between yin and yang has been disturbed. Chi Kung works by cleansing and energizing the meridian system and inner organs and restoring the feeling of health in both body and mind. Once chi is flowing freely again and our yin and yang energies are in balance, the body becomes more resilient to illness, disease and misfortune.

The focus of Chi Kung is the movement and redirection of chi. The moves are more static than those of Tai Chi, and both breathing and visualization techniques are used to circulate chi and rejuvenate our inner organs, or to send healing chi energy to particular parts of the body.

Chi Kung therapy is used widely in Chinese hospitals and has achieved resounding success in accelerating recovery from surgery and in curing life-threatening illnesses. Dr Hong Liu is a medical doctor and a Chi Kung master who specializes in curing cancer. Each cancer, AIDS or other seriously ill patient is prescribed healing Chi Kung exercises and herbal medicine with chemotherapy and medical drugs as part of an individual healing plan. In his book *Mastering Miracles*, he stresses that we must participate in our own healing no matter how ill or incapacitated we may be.

How to Practise Chi Kung

Balancing the Mind for Practice

The advantages and benefits of meditation can never be explained to a person who has never experienced it. Being constantly subjected to and stimulated by the excesses of our everyday world is a primary cause of mental and emotional stress. Most of us are completely unaware of how seriously disturbing and stressful to the mind and body is the daily noise from radios, TVs, road traffic and telephones. Stress severely damages the inner health of the body, therefore daily practice of exercises that can reduce the incessant chatter of the mind and relax and rejuvenate the body is hugely beneficial. The natural breathing pattern which keeps the inner systems balanced and in harmony has, in most adults, been disturbed or disorientated through stress or constant expression of negative emotions. Concentration on breathing, or some form of guided imagery, can help to harness the inner mental disturbances and retrieve physical order and stability.

Learning to breathe naturally again can be our own personal insurance policy for prevention of stress and physical disease. In stressful times, becoming immediately fully aware of our breathing gives us a moment to detach and take personal responsibility for our own health and well-being. Exercises such as Hara Breathing (page **167**), Modified Head Balance (page **168**), Straw Breathing (page **169**) or 'Using the Breath to Concentrate and Quieten the Mind' (page

171) can bring profound awareness of our breathing patterns and how quickly they respond to mindful attention. All of these exercises are ideal preparations for the principles of breathing in Tai Chi, Chi Kung, Yoga, Pilates or Feldenkrais. Once the breathing pattern has been regulated and returned to its natural rhythm, still meditation becomes easier and more accessible to a mind which is habitually consumed with internal conversation (see 'Breathing, Deep Relaxation and Meditation' exercises given in Chapter 3).

Breathing for Chi Kung Practice

During physical exercise it is most common to synchronize breathing with movement of the body. In Chi Kung practice, breathing is also synchronized with the movement of *energy*. This is achieved through single-minded concentration of the mind on breath and movement, which is essential so that both aspects remain flowing and connected. As soon as the mind is distracted by internal chatter, breathing falters, scattering and dissipating energy.

Visualization and mindful intention during practice of energy being drawn in and along the meridian channels or internal organs is said to have a resounding effect on healing inner organs, moving stagnant chi and generally rejuvenating the body's internal chi. Being able to recall clear images of how the inner organs look and where they are housed inside the body increases the intensity for and ability to heal internal disharmonies.

Breathing for Still Meditative Practice

The action of breathing is an energy which connects the mind and the body. When breathing becomes impaired, the body becomes heavy and sluggish, and the mind foggy and scattered. Although calming the mind through meditation alone will eventually relax the body, discomfort from residual physical stiffness and tension can initially interfere with the meditative process. For the majority of us, moving and stretching the body before still meditation practice is most beneficial. Physical exercise which incorporates specific breathing practices relieves, releases and relaxes the body, loosens the diaphragm, stimulates circulation and moves chi through the blood and meridian channels. As the body relaxes, the mind is also relieved from an outer layer of mental and emotional stress – allowing it to sink into a more restful and less disturbed state. Sitting quietly then becomes easier and more comfortable.

Three short sniffs through the nose to inhale, and three short blows through the mouth to exhale, practised for 1 or 2 minutes continuously, purify the bloodstream, invigorate the internal organs and bring mental clarity. This is of primary benefit when attempting to meditate. The sniffing breath practice – which is similar to Yoga's 'bellows breath' – can also be used when mental concentration and energy levels are low or flagging.

Basic Stance

The foundation for all Chi Kung practice begins (and is most often entirely executed in) Horse Stance. The feet are placed wider than hip-width to create a firm and stable framework for the exercises. For easy adjustment and balance during practice, it is important to lower the pelvic centre and extend the dan tien or Hara (as it is called in Japan) downward towards the earth by slightly bending the knees. The spine is elongated and the crown of the head is in alignment with the navel and the midpoint on the ground between the feet. The crown of the head extends up and away from the ground and navel. The head is considered to represent 'heaven', and the pelvis and feet 'the earth'. The Horse Stance promotes energy flow between these two points. Horse Stance is considered a most important posture in the practice of Chi Kung and all Chinese martial arts.

Posture

The main components of posture for the practice of Chi Kung exercises are:

1   **Head and Neck:** The head is balanced and held as if being lifted away from the shoulders. A lengthened neck, with the chin drawn in very slightly, aids neck alignment and ensures softness and relaxation of the throat muscles. Tension in the neck or throat impedes energy flow to the head, therefore being mindful of how the head is being held when changing direction is of the utmost importance during Chi Kung.

2   **Chest and Shoulders:** Concentration on the heart area allows the chest to open and expand naturally. Visualizing the heart lifting during practice draws the thoracic spine (middle back area) into the centre of the body, frees the diaphragm for breathing and contributes to overall awareness of spinal alignment. When attention is placed on lifting the heart area, the shoulders will usually relax and find their natural

alignment. However, slightly rounding the shoulders (without collapsing or hollowing the chest) broadens and softens the middle of the back, reducing the risk of tension being held there.

3   **Abdomen:** Abdominal or diaphragmatic breathing is practised in both Tai Chi and Chi Kung. The abdomen swells or distends during inhalation, and flattens or is compressed during exhalation (see Hara Breathing on page **167**). Good abdominal tone is essential for healthy diaphragmatic action when expelling air and gases from the body via the lungs. Strengthening the abdominal muscles greatly enhances our breathing. Body Conditioning exercises are ideal for developing good abdominal strength and tone (see Body Conditioning section in Chapter 3: pages **129–150**).

4   **Pelvis and Spine:** The pelvis is relaxed as if suspended between two poles – the hip joints. A slight tucking of the tail bone and bending of the knees transfers the body weight onto the thighs, which frees the lower back and hips. The spine then feels light, secure and supported in the Horse Stance posture.

5   **Knees:** When practising Chi Kung exercises for the first time, it is important not to bend the knees too deeply, particularly if you have a history of knee problems. In classical Chi Kung the toes are usually parallel. To reduce discomfort in the knees, turn the toes out at a 33-degree angle and press the knees (without forcing them) towards the little-toe side of the foot. This recruits strength and energy from the thigh muscles to support the knees and promotes overall stability of the upper leg.

6   **Feet:** Feet are hip-width apart and, as mentioned above, in classical training are parallel. Healthy, strong and correct alignment of the feet is considered to be essential for successful execution of postures, whether practising Tai Chi, Chi Kung or Yoga. Too much time spent in fashionable shoes (including athletic training shoes) severely weakens foot musculature. Strong feet keep us firmly connected to the ground. The old saying about having 'both feet firmly planted on the ground' describes someone who is self-directed, determined and with a good perspective on life. A sense of groundedness or connection with the earth, according to Yoga and Chi Kung philosophy, keeps the mind and emotions calm and stable. Masters of Yoga and Chi Kung also say that because of our 'fashionable habits' in the West we risk dying from our feet up. Once we lose the firm, stable foundation of our feet we begin losing strength and independence in life. Weakness in the feet causes weakness in the ankles, shins, knees, hips, pelvis, lower, mid- then upper spine, neck and head. According to these philosophies, agility and energy well into our more senior years are reliant on strong, flexible feet.

7   **Elbows and Hands:** Keeping all the joints of the body soft allows chi to travel unimpeded along the meridian channels. The inner elbow joint should be turned in towards the body, with the palms relaxed,

hollowed and facing backwards, fingers slightly curled. The Lao-gung points in the centre of the palms are considered the most powerful points in the body, from which energy can be transmitted.

8 **Eyes:** The gaze from the eyes should be soft. Focus on a point on the horizon or on the ground about 6 feet (2 metres) ahead; allow everything around that point to go slightly out of focus. Relax all the tiny little muscles behind the eyes and allow the eyeballs to drop deeper into the eye socket.

9 **Mouth:** Relax the jaw and the root of the tongue, and allow the throat to soften. The teeth may touch, but be aware of (and avoid) clamping or clenching the jaw.

10 **Tongue:** Placing the tip of the tongue on the roof of the mouth just behind the top teeth creates a closed circuit of energy, by connecting the two central channels in the body: the Governing and Conception Vessels (see page **15**). When practising Tai Chi, Chi Kung or Yoga postures, it is important to keep the tongue gently connected to the roof of the mouth so that internal chi or prana can be concentrated and then transported throughout the body.

Awareness of Chi

As chi energy is increased and begins to move through the systems, various sensations are experienced, from tingling, trembling or sweating to heat or cold. These sensations can occur in the extremities, abdomen, spine or the body as a whole. These physical experiences can be brought on by a combination of muscular responses to the exercises as well as indications that chi is opening up the energy system to move freely throughout the meridians and inner organs. As the body is nourished with breathing, movement and internal chi, circulation of both blood and chi improves, aiding elimination of toxic substances and bacteria, which can cause degeneration and disease in the body. Burping, coughing and flatulence during practice are indications of internal imbalances in the stomach, liver and digestive systems. With regular practice the system becomes healthier and these symptoms begin to subside. As with any other exercise discipline, warming-up and cooling-down exercises prevent muscle soreness. Gentle stretches before and after practice prepare and then settle the body and chi.

The Eight Precious Exercises of Chi Kung

It is impossible to find spirit without integrating the experience of the body.

Kenneth S. Cohen, *The Way of Qi Gong*

Sometimes referred to as the eight *brochades*, these exercises balance the yin and yang energies, prevent or eliminate disease and are prescribed to every patient by Chi Kung masters as the route back to health and vigour. In their full form these eight exercises unblock, cleanse and rejuvenate all of the main meridian channels. The Horse Stance (feet spread out slightly more than hip-width apart with the knees well bent), or variations on it, is the position from which all other exercises are practised. The full weight of the body in this stance is carried by the legs and feet, which is where all main meridians either begin or end.

Chi Ball and Chi Kung

In the Chi Ball Method these eight brochades have been adapted into moves which, with or without the ball, promote correct breathing and encourage the flow of chi through the body.

For more information on Chi Kung's eight precious exercises, see the Recommended Reading/ Further Resources section on page **206**.

Chi Ball Aerobic Dance

Inspired in the main by Tai Chi and Chi Kung, each Chi Ball Aerobic Dance move stretches, tones and cleanses the meridians (as will be demonstrated later in this chapter). As the entire body is engaged in the vigorous yet fluid movements, which vary in pace, size and direction, the session becomes in essence an interplay between yin and yang energies:

Body Movement		Chi Ball Aerobic Dance Move	
Yin	Yang	Yin	Yang
down	up	Sunset	Sunrise
left	right	Around-the-World Left	Around-the-World Right
backwards	forwards	The Mistral	The Swallow
sitting	standing	Seated Energy Row	Moving Energy Row
soft, slow	fast, energetic	Push-the-Wind	Ocean Wave
small movements	large movements	The Breeze	The Storm
upper body	lower body	The Space Roll	The Wind
front of the body	back of the body	The Mermaid	The Cobra
internal body	external body	Pelvic Circles	Circle-the-Sun
deep relaxation	full energy	The Fish Drape	Thunderbolt

The corresponding but opposing nature of the movements, which are large and small, forward and back, up and down, mirror the relationship between yin and yang. Correct breathing during the exercise generates chi, revitalizing and rebalancing the meridians.

The Chi Ball (where used) acts as a tool to focus the mind on the purpose of each move and helps us to become aware of the position of the meridians in our bodies.

Chi Ball Aerobic Dance Moves

The name and nature of each move reflects an element of the natural world. All moves are joined together in a class by basic aerobic dance choreography, such as marching, stepping side to side, or doing the Latin-style mambo step, making the format more familiar. Of the 18 moves listed below, we will be working in this book with no more than 10 (indicated by an asterisk [*]), which is the number used in a typical class.

Name	Chi Ball Aerobic Dance Move	Meridian
* Around-the-World	'grapevine'; pass the ball behind the back	Lung and large intestine
* Ocean Wave	wave arm back and forth in front of the body	Triple Heater, small intestine, large intestine
* Lightning	step, touch; pull elbow down/reach over head	Gallbladder
* Rainbow	syncopated step-touch; extend Chi Ball overhead to other side of the body	Gallbladder
* The Swallow	one step forward/two 'walks'; arms out to the sides ('horizon arms')	Lung and large intestine
* The Storm	step/squat; drop arm down/open overhead	Spleen/stomach, liver/gallbladder
* Sunset	step to side/squat; horizon/hold Chi Ball in both hands	Bladder, pericardium, Triple Heater
* Sunrise	straight legs/squat; raise Chi Ball above head/back to chest	Bladder, heart, Triple Heater
* Half-Moon/ * Full Moon	step, tap/step together; swinging arms side to side/full circle	Large intestine
The Exchange	step, touch; switch Chi Ball from hand to hand	Triple Heater, pericardium (heart constrictor)
The Horizon	arms straight and stretched to side from shoulders; round back; change ball to other hand; stretched to side lifting chest	Lung
Tilt the Horizon	step to side with right leg/drag left leg to close; ball in right hand/tilt shoulders and arms 45º	Lung, pericardium
The Breeze	mambo; internal/external rotation of shoulder	Liver (helps release anger and restores balance to the heart)
Thunderbolt	narrow 'V' step; squat/rise onto toes	All meridian points in the feet, energizing the central nervous system, strengthening the skeletal system and improving circulation
Sirocco	'V' step; hold Chi Ball/circle arms in front	Liver, gallbladder, large and small intestine, Triple Heater
The Pendulum	one step sideways/two 'walks'; reach arms out to the side	Liver

Name	Chi Ball Aerobic Dance Move	Meridian
The Mistral	alternating 'V' step; scoop arms forward/horizon	Bladder, stomach
The Wind	stationary: hold Chi Ball in both hands/move ribcage side to side	Gallbladder

How to Practise Chi Ball Aerobic Dance

Posture and Exercise Form

As with Tai Chi and Chi Kung exercises, keep the heart lifted in the upright moves or when returning from a downward movement. Be conscious of suspending the upper body from the hips and making space between all of the joints by fully expanding and lengthening the arms, legs and torso.

Rhythm and Flow

Use inspiring (non-vocal) music and allow your body to respond intuitively to the musical rhythms. Repetitive practice will inevitably result in graceful and effortless movement. Breathing and moving with continuous rhythmic flow increases the circulation of blood and chi, which warms and relaxes the body, bringing a calm and balanced state of mind.

Space

As you try each move, create space around you. By extending and expanding the body with movement, you create space *inside* the body in which all the inner organs can move and stretch to their optimal level.

Breathing

Use counting to regulate your breathing. Count the number of steps there are in each move. If it takes four counts to execute a move, inhale for two and exhale for two.

Yoga

If you look after the root of the tree, the fragrance and flowering will come of itself.
If you look after the body, the fragrance of the mind and spirit will come of itself.

B K S Iyengar

The word Yoga comes from Sanskrit, one the oldest known languages, often referred to as the mother of all others. The closest to Yoga in English is 'yoke', meaning 'a joining together or union', which in practice is what the discipline attempts to achieve. By working the mind, body and spirit simultaneously to restore balance to each, we can again become united in ourselves and with our world.

Yoga is believed to have been developed through spiritual practice in India more than 5,000 years ago. In its physical form it is the discipline upon which all other exercises have been based. In fact, the Hatha Yoga poses known as the Warrior, Hero, Triangle, Pyramid, Plank and Cobra are, in various forms, used in many aerobic classes today, the main difference being the speed at which they are performed.

The earliest written explanation of Yoga was provided by Patanjali in the 2nd century BC. He divided the discipline into eight stages or limbs (the last three of which require years of practice to achieve), which form the basis of most classes and Yoga theory today. These *Yamas* and *Niyamas* (moderation and behaviour respectively) provide a design for life as well as for practising Yoga, so as to get the maximum benefit from both.

The Foundations of Yoga Practice

Asanas – postures or poses

The aim in the physical practice of Yoga is to unite the mind and body. Unlike our everyday spontaneous movements, when working with the asanas we are forced to think about our breathing and have to concentrate on the body. To get the body and mind working together in this way is both relaxing and energizing: the release of built-up tension is a relief and provides a new source of vibrancy.

🔅 Pranayama – breath control

Prana means 'breath, life, energy and strength'; *ayama* means 'length, expansion, stretching and restraint'. Pranayama refers to the extension and control of our breath, through which we increase the levels of oxygen in the blood, provide the cells and organs with more nutrients and bring calm to the nervous system and muscles.

🔅 Pratyhara – controlling the senses

By learning to focus the mind and body in Yoga we become less vulnerable to distractions and better able to concentrate in all that we do.

🔅 Djarana – concentration

Our thoughts have great influence over the way we feel about ourselves. If we have more power over our thoughts we will be less likely to indulge those that can make us feel unhappy, angry, frustrated or negative in any other way.

🔅 Dhyana – meditation

Perhaps the very essence of Yoga, dhyana is where the body, breath, senses, mind and spirit become and function as one. This is achieved by uninterrupted concentration on nothing but the present moment, forgetting all past worries or fears for the future, and is most commonly referred to as meditation. To accomplish this is to experience detachment from an integration with the world and the self simultaneously. The nearest sensory description of being in this state is *bliss*.

🔅 Samadhi – self-realization

This means going beyond consciousness and is the ultimate aim of practising Yoga. Very few reach it, but those who have say any self-realization is a feeling of unutterable happiness.

The practice of Yoga and its benefits, summarized by Pranayama, or the controlled flow of our energy through the breath, occurs along a set of pathways in the body known as *nadirs*. The seven points at which these nadirs cross are called *chakras*, located from the crown of the head to the base of the pelvis. Our health is determined by the balance within each chakra. Assuming a sequence of poses (a series of positions) in Yoga penetrates every muscle, organ cell and bodily tissue, making it an effective natural form of stress relief. Regular practice also acts in ways similar to preventative medicine – the body with supple limbs, strong muscles, massaged vital organs and a stretched spine is less susceptible to damage or illness.

The Purpose of Yoga

Balance

We can often encounter injury, pain and discomfort if our body is asymmetrical. With regular Yoga practice comes enhanced co-ordination and physical awareness, with which we can gradually correct any imbalance between left and right, front and back, top and bottom of the body.

The Skeleton

Yoga postures correct alignment, loosen the joints and release pressure from the discs between our vertebrae by engaging the spine in all directions. These manoeuvres encourage strength and flexibility in what is the foundation bone of the body, the spine.

The Muscles

Slow, stretching Yoga postures stimulate the circulation and prevent the build-up of lactic acid (a potentially dangerous effect, which occurs when the muscles are not given enough time to relax after exercise) and help to correct poor posture by releasing the tension held in the muscles, making them appear leaner and longer.

The Nerves

Yoga helps remove toxins, increase neuro-transmissions (the connections between brain cells, affecting the muscles and other parts of the body) and stabilizes our physical reactions to stress, so reducing feelings of anxiety, a heart rate that is too high and physical effects such as sweating and muscular tension.

Endocrine (the Glands)

The body's production of hormones can be regulated by practising Yoga, which helps to cleanse the glands and stabilize the metabolism.

Respiratory/Cardiovascular

Yoga strengthens the heart, massages the lungs so their capacity is enhanced, and allows the bronchioles in the lungs, which might be congested, to maintain their elasticity.

Lymphatic/Immune System

The immune cells become stronger and therefore better able to fight infection. In stimulating the lymph glands, Yoga helps the body tissues to drain of toxins.

Mind/Emotions

Greater clarity and enhanced concentration make for inner strength and a sense of calm. Such sensitivity gives us an instinct for knowing what is right both in our practice of Yoga and in everyday life.

The Benefits of Particular Poses

Forward Bends

By stretching and therefore lengthening the entire back of the body, forward bends improve circulation and release tension through the feet, legs, spine and neck. As the space between each vertebra is increased in this movement, the nerves in the spine are nourished and the abdominal (stomach) muscles are massaged. The opening out of the chest, abdominal organs and pelvis in backward bends releases energy trapped in blockages of the heart and sex chakras. Such blockages occur either because of a lack of love or some other emotional trauma. While giving us a feeling of vitality, this movement also maintains a strong and supple spine.

Headstands and Shoulderstands

These positions increase the flow of blood to the head which, by activating the pineal and pituitary glands that regulate the body's chemical balance, improves our ability to think. The lymph glands are cleansed more efficiently by these postures, our digestion and waste-removal systems are enhanced, and insomnia, if a problem, is eliminated.

Twists

Twisting the body releases tension and therefore any aches or pains in the back, head, neck and shoulders. The small muscles in the spine that link the vertebrae are made stronger and the kidneys and abdominal organs re-stimulated.

Standing Postures

The mobility of our feet, hips, torso, spine, abdomen, chest, shoulders, arms and neck are all increased in standing postures, which provide a firm base of support for the spine. In this way we develop strength, endurance and greater flexibility throughout the body.

Hatha Yoga

Hatha Yoga (of which there are a now a number of variations) simply means physical Yoga. The *ha* refers to 'the sun, its passion, energy, activity, creativity and positively', while *tha* means 'the moon, which is cool, reflective, and negative'. Once again we see in the polarities a reflection of the yin/yang cycle; the nature of each posture in Hatha Yoga, whether it is yin or yang, ensures that our body is brought back to balance. Each posture has a counterpart to ensure the body is returned to a state of balance. And each pose is either yin or yang in nature.

The postures and exercises in Hatha Yoga are designed to balance our chi by guiding it into our organs, glands, joints, muscles and nerve fibres. With correct breathing and when executed in a slow and controlled manner, the postures help with the elimination of toxins and strengthen and cleanse the entire body.

General Benefits

Standing Postures

These develop emotional balance, poise, confidence and determination and improve strength and flexibility in the spine, shoulders, chest, hips, knees, ankles and feet.

Forward Bends

These stretch and lengthen the back of the body, release tension from the feet, legs, back and neck, and improve our circulation. Bending forward in Yoga also creates space between the vertebrae, which helps stimulate and nourish the entire nervous system. Forward bends massage the abdominal organs, aiding the entire digestive process too.

Backward Bends

These open and stretch our shoulders, chest and abdominal organs, thereby helping correct poor postural habits. The strength and flexibility of the spine is increased and our productive organs are nourished. Releasing both this area and the heart disperses emotional blocks, leaving us with more vitality and energy.

Inversions – The Bridge, the Plough, Shoulderstands and Headstands

Please note: These must *not* be done by women who are menstruating or pregnant.
By stimulating the pineal and pituitary glands in the brain, inversions help to chemically rebalance the body. They also promote clearer thinking and more stable emotions by increasing the blood flow to the head, alleviate insomnia and improve the drainage of our lymphatic system.

Twists or Spinal Rotation

These strengthen small but deep layers of muscle, stimulate the kidneys and abdominal organs and release tension. The nervous system is toned, while stiffness or pain in the back, head, neck or shoulders is relieved.

Chi Ball and Yoga

In the Chi Ball Method, Hatha Yoga is used for extension, balance and relaxation of the body. Pushing, reaching and stretching (with or without the ball in the hand) into some of the classic Yoga postures stretches all the meridian lines and helps to elongate and rebalance every aspect of the body.

Body Conditioning

From being a sickly child in the 1920s, German-born Joseph Pilates went on to become a proficient gymnast, diver and skier. By practising Yoga, Zen philosophy and Greek and Roman regimens he devised the Pilates Physical–Mind Method, which he used to reverse his own ill-health.

The very controlled and precise exercises Joseph Pilates developed focus on the use of the inner and outer abdominals, the mid-back muscles, the gluteals and the legs and arms to develop a core strength which stabilizes the spine and pelvis and helps us to gain an awareness of how our limbs function. Through practice, our strength, flexibility and posture are improved.

Practising Body Conditioning

Pilates® is a much-talked-about mind/body conditioning technique, in part because of the results achieved by those who practise it. Control of the body during any movement is the central focus of Body Conditioning (my development of Joseph Pilates' techniques), so a desire to understand how the body works and compensates for imbalance and poor postural habits is required.

Most of us will be unaware that through incorrect sitting and standing habits we have lost the use of our natural neuromuscular rhythms, which guide the safe timing, balance and control of our movements.

The lack in many of today's sports and exercise regimes of slow, controlled conditioning which fully engages our core muscles can compound the problem, leaving the body imbalanced. Because it works on the inner as much as the outer layer of muscle to avoid such imbalance and develop the body's physical strength, Body Conditioning can be used to rediscover movement skills and build power in a whole range of training disciplines.

It is also for this reason that many physiotherapists and osteopaths around the world are adapting the techniques to rehabilitate patients suffering sports or other work-related injuries. Research has shown that although the pain may subside from an aching back, for example, the essential stabilizing muscles never fully recover. Using Body Conditioning, the natural neuromuscular rhythms that protect the body from danger and injury in the way that it moves can be re-established and spinal health reinstated.

Breathing for Body Conditioning

Our natural patterns of breathing are often upset by negative emotions, which exacerbate bad postural habits. Our posture and muscle movement in general can be changed and enhanced by re-learning how to breathe. To begin with this can be difficult, but it is essential for the effective practice of Body Conditioning.

Breathing for Body Conditioning is very similar to that for Yoga, but the exhalation is done in three stages:

1   Soften the throat.

2   Drop the shoulders and feel the ribs funnel down towards your hips.

3   Flatten and widen the lower *rectus abdominus* (just above the pubic bone) by pressing the navel to the spine and drawing up the muscles of the pelvic floor.

During the final stage we should feel most stable, and this is when the movements of Body Conditioning are carried out. By focusing on exercises which immobilize the muscles attached to the pubic bone and the bottom of the ribcage (*rectus abdominus*), we can begin to practise postural stability. Through practice this method of breathing and attaining stability will become automatic and induce the same calm and relaxed sensation as correct breathing in Tai Chi, Chi Kung and Yoga.

Before practising the Body Conditioning exercises that follow, it is important that you bear in mind these points.

Alignment

Poor posture caused by too much sitting, slouching and stress has for most of us altered our skeletal structure, so before exercising we must find 'neutral spine' (see below). Although this is different for everyone, the best possible spinal alignment when sitting or standing is when the crown of the head is directly above the tail bone.

Neutral Spine

This is our natural spinal alignment, which very subtly forms the shape of an S (inward curve towards the lower end of our back, outward curve at the middle and another inward curve at the neck). This curve provides the natural elasticity necessary to absorb impact, stress and strain from daily activities such as climbing stairs, sitting and standing, lifting, carrying and even lying down. Because the rest of our body arranges itself according to the S in our spine, the health of our muscles, tendons and inner organs depends upon its being kept in good order.

Neutral spine

To find your own neutral spine, lie on the floor with your knees bent and place a hand underneath your lower back, just above the pelvis. You should feel a space there, and another under your neck. Once you have found your natural curve, try to retain the position during exercise.

Stabilizing the Torso

This can be done in two ways:

Scapular elevation

1   When lying supine with the knees bent:
Lengthen your neck and gently press the shoulders against the floor, then slide them down towards your hips to get a sense of stability across the upper back and shoulder blades (scapula depression, see picture).

Without arching the back, gently press the back of the pelvis (sacrum) down against the floor; lift your pubic bone very slightly and feel the lower back gently elongate. This is called 'imprinting' the pelvis.

Scapular depression

Breathe and slowly compress the abdomen against the spine without tilting the pelvis or allowing the lower back to press into the floor.

2   When kneeling on hands and knees (cat posture):

Push down into the palms, extending and lengthening the arms through the
elbows.

Retract the shoulders, drawing them away from the ears and towards
the hips.

Cat posture

Breathe, and on the exhalation compress the abdomen up against the
spine (this should take a minimum of five counts to complete).

Breathing

The breathing in Body Conditioning should come from the ribcage and muscles of the middle of
the back (thoracic spine). Because it assists movement, co-ordinating the breath during exercise
is essential. To practise correct breathing, stand in front of a mirror and firmly hold a towel that
has been wrapped round your ribcage. As you breathe in, see if you can push your ribcage
against the towel, then feel it loosen as you breathe out. It might be useful to do this six to eight
times before starting the exercises.

Concentration and Co-ordination

When our stabilizing muscles are weak it can be difficult to maintaining 'neutral spine', especially
when adding the movement of arms and legs to an exercise. Be aware and try to avoid the
following ways in which the body tries to compensate for weak stabilizing muscles:

When lying on the back the ribcage can push forward as the arms are raised above the
head, the sternum (chest) can collapse and the lower back (lumbar spine) flatten when a foot is
lifted off the floor, or the opposite hip bone of a leg being raised off the floor can dip.

When on all fours with one arm or leg raised above the head, the middle of the back rounds
up and the chest can cave in, the abdomen can drop and the lower back begin to arch, or
excessive weight may be transferred to the supporting arm or leg, leaving the back abnormally
overloaded.

Stamina and Control

This means maintaining 'neutral spine' as you begin to exercise. Most people, at some point, have either to let their correct posture or their breathing go. But with practice you will improve, and, once comfortable, exercising in neutral spine can further challenge the stabilizing muscles by the addition of weight, such as if you hold a dumbbell or a bottle or water.

Fluidity

All movements must be controlled and smooth to avoid making use of momentum, which tempts the body back into old, poor postural habits. When exercising, ensure that all the necessary muscles are engaged.

Precision

Less variation, slower movements and fewer repetitions done correctly will achieve far more than many repetitions with no control or concentration. To help develop an awareness of your ability to maintain the correct posture and the importance of precision during exercise, use the image of the Pelvic Clock:

Lie on your back and imagine the face of a clock on your pelvis.

- The pubic bone is 12 o'clock.
- The right hip bone is 3 o'clock.
- The top of the abdominal/base of the ribs is 6 o'clock.
- The left hip bone is 9 o'clock.

Body Conditioning and Chi Ball

In order mainly to address correct posture, the Chi Ball Method uses moves based on those developed by Joseph Pilates with other spinal rehabilitation techniques to build strength in the body's centre. In terms of our energy cycle (see page **9**), the movements in Body Conditioning reflect the Earth Element (Descending Yang), which is why it follows Yoga (Fire Element, Rising Yang) in a class.

Feldenkrais Method

Human movement in space is a communication ground between intentional movement out of conscious discernment and innate talent for spontaneous and effective self-organization.

Ruthy Alon, *Mindful Spontaneity*

Born in the Ukraine in 1904, Moshe Feldenkrais was an engineer, mathematician and physicist as well as a master of judo. After years of physical stiffness and a knee injury, incurred while competing for a European judo black belt, he set about studying all subjects related to human movement including kinesiology, physiology, neurology, anatomy and psychology, in an attempt to understand how to unlock the physical movement patterns into which he had become set and which were partly responsible for his injuries.

Through his study Feldenkrais developed a unique understanding of the working of the sensory-motor system (the internal mechanism within us that allows the brain to send messages to the muscles) and its link with our thoughts, actions and emotions.

He found that the progression of a child's motor skills were vital to the development of the brain. Lacking muscular strength, babies instinctively find the most effortless way to sit, crawl and stand using nerve stimuli within the muscles alone. As a baby's physical abilities progress, so do his or her mental faculties.

As we become adults and the body adapts to movement that is restricted largely to lying down, sitting and standing, our muscular flexibility declines. Poor postural habits change the way we move, and the effort required to do what as children we found easy gradually increases. As our muscular flexibility declines, the corresponding motor pathways in the brain via the central nervous system close down, leaving us stuck both in our ways of thinking and moving.

By replicating a baby and repeating movement patterns in their most basic form, Feldenkrais found that new connections between the motor cortex of the brain and the muscular system were made, therefore making it possible to reprogramme the central nervous system and retrain the body to move in a more energy-efficient manner. A body that moves in such a way uses less energy and is therefore stronger and more relaxed.

To reflect what he had learned from watching babies' physical progress, Feldenkrais exercises are largely conducted on the floor. Here the body is freed from the demands of gravity and the brain is freed from convention. Many people find their movements become slower, more introspective and sensitive, which immediately enhances their physical awareness, making the floor the idea place to rediscover how to move and become aware of pockets of tension and immobility.

Participants are encouraged to ignore matters of technique and precision, and encouraged instead to concentrate on using their bodies as a system rather than focusing on individual muscles. By rolling, rocking and stretching, we gradually rediscover long-forgotten movement patterns.

Because one of its effects is to preserve energy, Feldenkrais is a rejuvenating as well as a very relaxing exercise. Comparisons of the body 'before and after' often reveal significant shifts in posture and promote a greater awareness of incorrect postural habits.

Re-learning How to Move

Walking is a perfect example of how many of us become stuck in energy-inefficient patterns of movement. Covering long distances is often tiring and uncomfortable for us because our natural flow of walking has been blocked by poor posture either in the pelvis, back, knees or ankles, causing the body to feel stiff and sore.

We cannot correct poor posture by addressing just one element of bad walking technique; for effective, long-lasting change we must reprogramme the entire body. Feldenkrais uses a huge variation of movement sequences, repeated many times over, to re-establish for both the brain and body a whole new pattern of movement.

Because the body and brain respond more quickly to changes on one side at a time, Feldenkrais moves are often focused on either the left or right. The movements are slow and repetitive, as Feldenkrais himself believed that intense physical exercise was abusive, shocking the system and desensitizing the body.

How to Practise the Feldenkrais Method

Before trying to change the way you move, try first to establish which of your movement patterns are pre-set. The following exercises help build this awareness.

Crossing the Legs, Arms and Hands

Without thinking about it, sit on a chair or the floor and cross your legs. The leg you crossed first is the one you will automatically use because of a setting in your brain. Try the same with your arms: the same pattern should emerge. Now try clasping your hands. Which thumb is on top? Now unclasp your hand and try putting the opposite thumb on top.

Writing

The hand with which you write is established soon after your second birthday. As you write, are you aware of any other part of the body moving? Probably not. Because this action is so efficient, no unnecessary muscular movement is involved. Now switch hands and try to write. How difficult or awkward does this feel? The sensation will give you some idea of how it feels to try to engage an under-used and under-developed pattern of movement.

Cleaning Your Teeth

Notice how much of your body is engaged when trying to brush your teeth with the opposite hand. Again, this gives you a glimpse of the way in which an under-developed motor pathway from the brain to the muscle can impair movement.

To illustrate the effectiveness of Feldenkrais, 'before-and-after' exercise comparisons are extremely useful. The following body-mapping techniques can also help reveal which of our daily movement patterns are habits and how they can be made to change when the muscles are fed new information from the brain.

Walking

Walk around the room or garden and think about which part of your sole hits the ground first, how hard your feet impact with the floor, how your knees feel, whether your pelvis, spine or neck move and how solid your head feels on your shoulders. Now perform the Feldenkrais Chi Ball exercises Lean and Look, Side-Lying Pelvic Rock, Pelvic Tilting, Elevated Pelvic Tilting, Pelvic Circles and Elevated Pelvic Circles (beginning on page **151**), then walk again, noticing how different it feels.

Lying on Your Back

Lie flat with straight legs slightly apart and the palms turned up, 6 inches (15 centimetres) away from the sides of your body. Scan your body, registering how much of your back is in contact with the floor, how even (or uneven) your legs and hips feel, whether the shoulder blades feel under pressure and how much space there is between the lower part of your back and the floor. Now perform the Feldenkrais Chi Ball exercises Pelvic Circles, Pelvic Tilting, Neck Circles and Modified Fish (beginning on page **155**) and see if there is a difference when you lie flat once again.

Twisting

Sit down sideways on a chair, so its back is next to your right arm. Holding the sides of the chair, gently turn and see how far you are able to twist. Do the Feldenkrais Chi Ball exercises Side-Lying Shoulder Rock, Side-Lying Pelvic Rock and Butterfly Twists (beginning on page **151**). Now return to the chair and twist again. Is it easier? Can you twist further? Are you making less of an effort? Does the movement feel entirely more comfortable? The answer to all of these should be yes.

Bending Forward

With the knees slightly bent, try to touch your toes. (If you have back pain do this from a chair with the legs hip-width apart.) Notice how hard this feels or how stiff your legs are. Perform the Feldenkrais Chi Ball exercise Lean and Look (page **160**). Now repeat the bend and see if it feels any easier. Hold the bend for a while and try to detect any other movement in the spine, back muscles or legs. Can you feel bones or muscles you were completely unaware of before the exercise?

Lateral Stretching

Either standing with the feet wide apart or sitting in a chair, bend over to the right and raise your left arm above your head. How do the waist, ribcage, shoulder and neck feel? Now do the Feldenkrais Chi Ball exercise Side Lift and Look (page **161**), lying on the left side first. Then perform the seated exercises to the right. Repeat the lateral stretch and see if the move requires less strain or feels any more natural.

These exercises give you an idea of your potential for change, although just as with any other type of exercise several sessions will be needed before alterations in your movement habits become noticeable and sustainable. These exercises can be modified to be more gentle when energy needs to be conserved.

The following 10 points are also worth bearing in mind to benefit most from the exercises based on the Feldenkrais Method:

1   Pick a theme. Choose a Chi Ball exercise with a focus on either moving sideways, forwards, twisting or walking and see how many variations on it you can create and how supple you feel after practising them.

2   Begin on one side. Start exercising one part of one side of the body, such as the right arm, or left leg, repeating and varying the move, and only gradually integrating the rest of the body.

3   Move the more flexible side first. This makes the entire exercise more enjoyable. By the time you come to work on the stiffer side, the whole body is warmer and more supple.

4   Go for skill, not effort. Pamper yourself with exercise – how you do it is much more important than how hard you feel you are working.

5   Observe the breathing. The more integrated the breathing with the movement, the more pleasurable and effective it will be.

6   The pleasure principle. Do not force yourself to persevere too much, for too long, with moves you find hard and dislike. You are far more likely to give up entirely if you do.

7   Be detached and aware. Listen to your body. Do not be driven by achieving quick results.

8   Relax. The more relaxed you are, the easier the moves will be and the clearer it will become to sense any resistance.

9   Focus on movement, not muscle. Muscular effort should not be needed during these moves.

10   Vary the speed. Experiment with slow moves to build awareness, and fast moves to develop ability.

Feldenkrais and Chi Ball

Feldenkrais techniques in Chi Ball are used to increase awareness of the way we move, but also to reintroduce into exercise the idea of playfulness, which helps us relax. Checking posture before and after each exercise reveals an increased range of movement, so, as with any game we like to win, it also gives a feeling of achievement and satisfaction. It hardly needs adding that the benefits of disentangling the body from years of inefficient movement patterns are immense, including greater strength, flexibility and more energy.

Deep Relaxation

Our ability to relax reflects our willingness to trust.

Anonymous

The final component to living a happy balanced life is to balance the mind. Today there is an abundance of information and methods available to teach us about the ideal way to be, along with the diets which promise an ideal body in 10 days or less. They purport to be the answer to all our problems and the unhappy circumstances in which we find ourselves.

Achieving balance in our lives takes practice. Stress and personal drama is a habit. We have to re-learn how to be and how to sustain a calm and relaxed state. Learning anything in life has always been effective for me when I have been given clear and concise stages of learning. Greatly valued and appreciated teachers have given me clear signposts and indicators of progress or potential hiccoughs that may crop up along the way. Many people abandon their relaxation and meditation practice because they decide that it's not 'doing' anything much for them. They have not achieved the state promised in the book, seminar or workshop.

First of all, I believe it is vitally important to inform people of the reasons for participating in a chosen practice. Many workshops or retreats can leave the first-time attendee a little confused and abandoned in their experiences. Retreats where meditation is taught, particularly, often do not result in the promise of post-euphoric mindful states. Numerous people have found the experience alarmingly confronting and painful, because once the mind becomes deeply relaxed and the hold on our negative emotions are loosened all sorts of past memories will begin bubbling up to the surface requesting expression and release. Some of these experiences can be quite shocking, and if the retreat leaders are not enlightened or compassionate enough to nurture and support people during these emotional states, the memory of the original experience might be snapped back into place and the valuable opportunity for its release may be lost.

Having clear information which supports and carries us through encourages most of us to continue persevering with the journey. We all need goals and indicators of progress to affirm and congratulate ourselves as we progress. This part of the Chi Ball Method is subtle but the most profound. The goal is finally to let go and surrender to the part of ourselves that knows the whole story about life and who we really are in relation to it. It is in this state that, as the masters say, we will find our true nature, which is sheer bliss. It is in this state that the body and our lives can more easily be healed.

The journey to being free from stress, tension and fatigue can be approached in three stages: Breathing, Deep Relaxation and Meditation.

By returning to a natural rhythm of breathing the first band of tension is freed from the mind and body, making it easier for us to practise Deep Relaxation.

Deep relaxation provides the experience and practice we need in order to relax fully in preparation for meditation.

Meditation is the final stage for bringing balance and tranquillity to the mind.

Breathing

The breath is the key to your emotional state because it both reflects and can control your level of tension.

Dan Millman

Improving the way we breathe to increase our daily oxygen intake can only enhance the performance of our immune system. How we breathe is also an indication of the degree to which we suppress or express our feelings.

Emotional stability is dependent upon our ability to breathe a full, natural diaphragmatic breath. Full deep breathing reveals an ease with our lives, while breathing that is short and shallow shows we are tense. The expanding and contracting motions of breathing are interlinked with and can act as a barometer of our ability to cope with whatever happens to us in our life. Think about the way you draw in breath when given a fright, and then sigh when relieved.

We are born with the correct breathing ability, which is right from the lower abdomen, allowing the diaphragm to expand fully. When we are stressed, breathing is the first thing to be affected. Recent surveys show that in Britain alone more than 267,000 days of work are lost each year due to stress-related illness.

The most common breath response to stress is called 'reversed breathing' (also referred to as 'upper chest breathing'], caused by a fearful reaction to life's circumstances. During natural, healthy breathing the abdomen moves out and away from the body as we inhale and towards the body as we exhale. In reversed breathing the opposite occurs: the abdomen moves in as we breathe in, and out as we breathe out. Breathing this way severely overworks the secondary breathing muscles, causing immense tension in the head, facial muscles, neck, shoulders, upper back and chest.

Upper body breathing reduces the amount of air that the lungs can potentially receive. Our breath rate or number of exhalations per minute will increase to compensate for the reduced amount of air entering the lungs. This, on a subtle level, will also cause stress to the heart. When the upper body is forced to perform the breathing action, our ability to take air into the lungs is impaired. The brain and heart need enormous amounts of oxygen to function, therefore poor breathing habits will severely affect these organs. Signs of an impaired breathing pattern which are regularly linked with stress are emotional instability, a rapid heartbeat, high blood pressure, muscular aches and pains, migraines, lethargy and fatigue.

Re-learning to breathe deeply and diaphragmatically cleanses our air sacs of pollutants by allowing more oxygen to reach the lungs and replace stale air collected there by shallow breathing. Ancient Eastern exercise disciplines such as Yoga, Tai Chi and Chi Kung work on the basis that without correct breathing a strong immune system, a calm mind and stable emotions are almost impossible to sustain. Masters of these ancient disciplines breathe between five and six times a minute, compared to the average person, who breathes 14 to 18 times a minute. This enables them to remain calm yet mentally alert at all times. According to TCM, only when you can properly control your breathing can you effectively control your life.

Emotions and Our Breathing Patterns

Emotions are best understood as unexpressed feelings or blocked energy that takes refuge somewhere in the body. Clinical tests have shown that when we put a person under severe stress the fight or flight response is triggered. We would assume that the fearful reaction would cause the whole body to experience the fear. This is not the case. The reaction to the stress felt is habitually exaggerated in a particular location in the body depending upon the individual, probably leading to a problem in that area sometime in the future. For some people the digestion is affected.

For others, the lower back, neck or shoulders register the stress. This falls in line with the philosophy of Yoga and Traditional Chinese Medicine that suppressed emotion will affect and injure us internally.

Unencumbered by any particular mode of behaviour, children will freely cry, scream and shout as a way of communicating their feelings. As adults we tend to hold on to feelings of sadness, fear, anxiety, frustration and disappointment which, when not expressed, cling to the body and over time disrupt our natural breathing pattern and weigh down our entire system.

The breathing exercises in Yoga, Tai Chi and Chi Kung help to free the body of the habitual tension that keeps negative thoughts and emotions trapped inside the body. We become detached and distanced from our thoughts and experiences instead of fully feeling, owning and integrating our entire being, including the negative and positive experiences which make us all unique and special. Breathing helps us integrate and flow with our emotions instead of reacting to them.

The table below illustrates which unexpressed emotions are linked with particular breathing patterns.

Emotion	Breath Response
Fear	Light, shallow (upper chest)
Anger/Frustration	Weak inhalation, forced exhalation (deep sighing)
Sorrow/Grief/Sadness	Jerky inhalation, weak or faint exhalation

Most of us give no thought to how we breathe or the way in which the body reacts to it. Muscular tension can also inhibit our breathing by restricting the natural movement of the diaphragm. The secondary breathing muscles then take over, and as a result are overloaded. To breathe properly is to allow the abdomen to move out as we inhale and shrink back as we exhale.

To learn how to breathe properly we must first become aware of any tension in the ribcage, chest, shoulders, neck, throat or face, and then learn how to release it. This is done with exercises that stretch and expand the ribcage and balance the muscular system, releasing tension and focusing the mind.

Meditation and Deep Relaxation ensure that old breathing patterns remain a habit of the past, and are excellent practices for re-establishing natural breathing patterns. The role of the breath is to slowly release long-term emotional 'holding patterns' to free the mind and relax the entire body. The inhalation in Eastern philosophy is said to activate, prepare and stir the mind, activate and prepare the body and metabolically nourish us on a cellular level. The exhalation settles, releases and calms the mind, relaxes the body and metabolically cleanses.

Correspondences	Breathing In	Breathing Out
The Mind	Stimulates, stirs, activates	Settles, releases, calms
The Muscular Body	Activates, prepares	Releases, relaxes
The Metabolic Body	Nourishes: millions of new cells are born	Cleanses: millions of dead cells are expelled

To change any poor habit we must first become aware that it exists. The following are very simple breathing exercises, which will help you become aware of your breathing and also introduce to you a way of breathing that may help disassemble a current detrimental breathing pattern. This will immediately relieve anxiety, stress or tension. Re-educating the breathing mechanism is hugely beneficial to your health and state of mind.

The purpose of these exercises is to improve flexibility in the ribcage, to free the diaphragm and relieve stress by reducing the breath rate (number of exhalations) per minute. Each exercise will promote breath awareness and will induce a calmer state of mind. It is very difficult to make the choice to implement change of any sort without experiencing a more pleasurable alternative to the current state being employed. These exercises are excellent preparations for Deep Relaxation and Meditation.

The Butterfly – see page **81**

Circle-the-Sun – see page **83**

Circle-the-Moon – see page **84**

Corpse Pose – see page **128**

Straw Breathing – see page **169**

Modified Head Balance – see page **168**

Deep Relaxation

Relaxation is the first step towards intuitive wisdom.

Wong Kiew Kit

Practising Deep Relaxation techniques is the second step towards reaching our natural state of being. Deep relaxation is really a willingness to soften and surrender every part of yourself and to completely let go of all tension in the mind and the body,. A majority of people have no idea how much tension they are carrying in their bodies.

A story about a Master of Aikido teaching a student illustrates the point. In order to try to teach his pupil the meaning of true power and strength, at each lesson the Aikido Master would tell his pupil to relax. As time passed the preoccupation of the lessons remained the same until, hugely frustrated, the student told his teacher that after six months of practice he felt more tense than ever. How could he ever relax? The Aikido Master replied, 'It is only now that you are aware of your tension that I can begin to teach you.'

Balancing the Body

Most of us are uncomfortable with stillness and silence. The whole structure of a Chi Ball class or an exercise session at home is to release tension. As surface tension is released we are more willing and able to relax. To achieve this aim the Chi Ball is used to squeeze and massage large bands of tension from three commonly blocked energy points along the spine: the sacrum (back of the pelvis), thoracic spine (middle of the back just below the shoulder blades) and cervical spine (the top of the neck). When these energy points are stimulated and released, a pleasurable sense of relaxation is induced. Following these final sequences the ball is removed and we take time to lie completely still. This is the first time many of us have a glimpse of our natural state, which is completely still, calm and tranquil. In this state our bodies can heal more easily and we begin to reach that part of ourselves that knows deep inner joy, peace and contentment.

I often ask my students how often in their normal working day they feel like this? For those who have no experience of Meditation or Deep Relaxation, the answer is usually rarely to never. I then ask, if the answer is never, how far they deviate from this feeling in their daily lives?

The goal of Deep Relaxation is to become intimately connected to and familiar with this feeling of being deeply calm and relaxed, and then see how long you can sustain the feeling. A body and mind held in a straightjacket of tension, stress and dissatisfaction causes disease, ill-health and a weak immune system.

Building Awareness

Using 'before-and-after' comparisons with exercise makes us aware of pockets of tension and is a very easy yet powerful tool for gaining knowledge about ourselves. Noticing several times, for example, that there is stiffness in the neck and shoulders which is much relieved following exercise encourages us to question our daily habits. How am I sitting at work? Is my neck jutting slightly forward as I look at the computer screen? The head weighs 10 to 12 pounds (around $4^{1}/_{2}$ to $5^{1}/_{2}$ kilos), which pulls on the shoulder and neck muscles. Prolonged periods of sitting with poor posture causes great strain and discomfort. At any time we can all make the choice to become responsible for our own health and well-being.

Either stand still with your feet hip-width apart, sit comfortably on a chair with both feet flat on the floor and your back straight, or lie down on the floor with your legs straight and feet slightly turned out, arms and hands a few inches away from the body with palms up. Take a minute to scan your body and your mood before beginning your Chi Ball session. Begin at the soles of your feet and slowly work your way up the body. Notice your feet, ankles, calf muscles, thighs. Then feel the position of the pelvis. Are you aware of any tension in the hips and lower back? How does the whole of your back feel? Do the shoulders feel tense? Is your neck relaxed and free or does the weight of your head feel a burden to your neck? Now be aware of your mood. Do you feel tense, stressed, depressed? Or happy, peaceful and relaxed?

After your Chi Ball session, re-scan each area of your body and see if you notice any changes. Does one area feel lighter, heavier or more flexible than before? How is your overall mood? Do you feel more emotional than before? Is it a pleasant feeling or a little overwhelming? Often when we become fully relaxed, our mental and physical armour is dismantled. All sorts of fears, anxieties or long-term unexpressed emotions may bubble to the surface for release. Try not to judge, berate or criticize these feelings. In a sympathetic, kind, compassionate and detached manner, try to watch and observe the feelings – and, most importantly, continue breathing. Even go so far as to immerse yourself completely in the emotional wave and allow it to wash over you.

When we resist feeling blocked emotions fully, we feed them and increase their intensity. Allowing ourselves to feel and be fully present in the wave of emotional feeling is an opportunity to release the emotional tension which has been holding us prisoner for far too long. Keeping negative emotions stored inside us takes immense energy. This is the cause of much depression, lethargy, physical ailments, Chronic Fatigue Syndrome and many other illnesses. Our bodies become unique warehouses for storing emotional baggage. As I have travelled around the world presenting the Chi Ball Method, many, many people have ended the class in a tearful and emotional state. For many this is the first time in years that they have felt deeply relaxed – the state in which our feelings can rise to the surface.

Unfortunately our society teaches us not to show or express our emotions in public, and for most participants the opportunity to explore these feelings fully is cut short by timetables and schedules dictated by the conference or health centre. Initially, finding an environment which is safe and nurturing is vital in the first stages of relaxation and release. We also need to give ourselves permission to let go and flow with our feelings without judgement or opinion.

Meditation to Balance the Mind

Be empty, be still. Watch everything just come and go. Emerging from the Source – returning to the Source. This is the way of Nature. Be at peace. Be aware of the Source. This is the fulfilment of your destiny. Know that which never changes. This is enlightenment.

Lao Tzu, *Tao te Ching*

This is not intended to be read as intellectual material for entertainment or analysis, but rather as a guide to be referred to as, when and only if you decide to commit yourself to the practice of meditation. As the days pass, the material presented here may become relevant and, I hope, helpful.

Much has been written about meditation and, in the purest sense, this is a complete contradiction. Meditation is actually something that is very difficult to explain or write about, and Zen philosophy says meditation should not be written about. In the end you just have to do it to experience it. Describing, analysing and contemplating the advantages and disadvantages is to intellectualize it. Meditation cannot be successfully intellectualized, it can only be experienced.

All that said and done, I would still like to offer you in this book my own understanding, insights and experiences, which may encourage you to begin the practice of meditation.

Its rewards are profound and the reason I have included it as part of the Chi Ball Method is because meditation is, in the end, the most profound pathway to freeing the mind, body and spirit. The class itself is actually a preparation for the Deep Relaxation and Meditation phase; the various Tai Chi, Chi Kung and Yoga exercises release muscular tension between periods of sitting for meditation, enabling the mind and body to surrender in meditation without physical distraction.

Exercise will without doubt bring freedom to the body, and to a great degree also free the mind. But meditation is a process that may finally free the constraints which keep locked tight the secrets to true health and happiness. The following is an in-depth conversation about meditation, but for the purposes of the Chi Ball Method it is a stage to which you can progress whenever you feel ready and willing to take full responsibility for your whole life. This stage will bring us in closest contact with our spirit. It is the stage that may really tell us about ourselves and how and why we interact with our world the way we do.

It's Not about Them, It's about Us!

I have taught Deep Relaxation or Meditation on countless occasions in fitness centres around the world. Participants often complain that they are unable to relax because of excessively distracting loud music in another part of the building, or a group of people standing outside the room talking and laughing prevents them from being able to follow my instructions to let go and just be fully present in the moment. Each of us has to realize and accept that the loud distracting noise says more about us than about anything else. It is not about the disturbing noise. It's about our reaction to it. When there is discomfort or irritation, we need to learn to feel and accept the emotions these so-called disturbances are bringing up. The purpose of the practice of meditation is to feel and stay with the whole experience without judgement or comment.

Someone once told to me a story about a group of people who decided to spend time in a Buddhist retreat centre somewhere in southeast Asia. Next to the retreat centre was a factory which bellowed out loud noise and dreadful fumes throughout the day and night. By the third day a number of the group were incensed that they had travelled all that way for a peaceful retreat to practise meditation, only to be subjected to unbearable noise and pollution. Apparently the head monk listened politely, then said to them, 'This is the practice.' He then slowly stood up and left the room. Some ended up leaving, some of the group chose to stay. The point of this story is that when we need our lives, environment or circumstances to be a certain way in order to feel good, we normally avoid fully experiencing and feeling. Anger at the noise from the factory was an opportunity for these people to sit and feel their anger and practise just being in that situation with no opinions or judgements. 'The practice' is about experiencing everything life deals us as part of the whole of life. We experience only a portion of life when we need everything to be a certain way. When a circumstance causes us drama, pain or distress we immediately blame the person, incident or situation.

Reasons for Mental and Emotional Imbalance

When we perceive situations, circumstances or people as the cause of our pain and distress, we remain trapped in our pain. Reliving, again and again, these scenarios can take us to a point where we are most likely to become completely dissociated from and refuse to deal with the cause of our repeating personal crisis.

Dissociation from our experiences can manifest as childish behaviour and temper tantrums, moodiness, depression, a minor withdrawal or even a major nervous breakdown. Until we all realize that the anger, sadness or distress we feel is built on a memory of having been subjected to a situation in the past when a parent or someone else may have shouted at us in a threatening manner, or that we have been injured, reprimanded, humiliated or abandoned by someone, we began to perceive that life was not a safe place to be. These are experiences forced upon us. Our mind can become fragmented through many negative experiences of the past, which can result in us closing down and 'dissociating' ourselves from the experiences.

Some experiences may have been so painful that we decided to separate and detach ourselves completely from any memory of them. This is called a blocked emotional experience. Pain that is not felt and integrated into our state of being seems to be stored, instead, somewhere in the physical body. It may contribute to a lifetime of back pain, knee problems, migraines, poor digestion, high blood pressure, cancer or numerous other physical symptoms.

Why Meditate?

Meditation is about the effortless integration of the flow of emotional feeling and being.

Anonymous

Learning to meditate may be the best gift you could ever give yourself. Meditation and Deep Relaxation, with time and practice, can release the hold your negative habits and emotions have over you and free you from the causes of conflict, stress, unhappiness and your own private emotional roller coaster. Initially, meditation can make you exceedingly uncomfortable. As you sit in silence for the first time you may feel as if your world is being tipped upside down. Memories and feelings begin moving along the hidden corridors of the mind and come forward for recognition and release. Acupuncturist Michael Porter said to me once that the early stages of meditation can be similar to putting a high-pressure hose into the middle of a garbage bin. Most of what comes up can be smelly, rotten and completely unpalatable, and probably no longer useful to us as a basis for our emotional life.

There are many descriptions of what to expect or what one should do in meditation. The secret is to expect nothing and do nothing. When you meditate you are not actually doing anything, you are practising how to *be*. Be with yourself, be quiet, be still, be aware, be patient, be relaxed and be fully awake to your experiences. Being is the most basic element of our experience and the most important one. Being here now frees us of fear.

The objective of meditation is to regain your vulnerability, which means to be sensitive and open-hearted. Being vulnerable does not mean weak. On the contrary, the goal is to become a fearless warrior who feels anything and everything life presents, and to be fully awake to the whole experience. The definition of weakness in this instance is when you avoid your feelings and place blame on the outside world and those around you for the circumstances in which you find yourself.

Meditation can reintegrate your soul or spirit, and retrieve the lost pools of attention caused by unfavourable experiences in your childhood. Inability to recall childhood memories and experiences means that your feelings and memories are fragmented in the brain. The purpose of meditation is to return us all to the state of sheer pleasure experienced in infancy which is unfettered by comment or opinion, and regain the magic of being truly awake in each present moment. Meditation re-empowers the imagination, unlocks lost gifts and brings the magic back into ordinary moments. When we lose touch with our process of experiencing, we become lost in materialism. We become wooed and sold on ideas which tell us that true bliss and happiness in life requires a special formula of wealth, possession or power as seen in Hollywood.

Our schooling teaches us to postpone or save up for future pleasure: 'Deny yourself now, work hard and save up so that you can enjoy your success later.' We begin thinking along the lines of, 'Life would be wonderful if only I can pass my exams, score that good job or get that promotion.' Yet just as one goal is met there seems to be another one popping up in an endless stream, with 'the good life' always tantalizingly just out of reach, requiring a more and more complex formula as we get older until finally we focus on our retirement. Reinforcement of this much-advertised illusion of future fulfilment at a price is continuous. If only we could afford that Mercedes car, new penthouse or the around-the-world trip, then we could feel truly alive! We forget that, long ago, we have made a conscious decision not to feel bliss here and now, nor to see the utter magic that surrounds us in the ordinary moments of our lives.

Our emotional state becomes governed by factors outside our control. We are taught to think that our problems are external factors which we must control. Meditation teaches you that it all comes from the inside, that you internally make choices. Eventually, through meditation you realize that you are in fact the master of your own feelings. 'I am feeling this way because I choose to feel this way' – this secret you may never own until you choose to meditate. In your darkest moments, friends who may tell you this may be seen as your worst enemies. Meditation can help you find your key to unlock the secret to realizing that you have given permission to your perceived enemies who are 'making' you feel angry, upset, fearful or disempowered.

Freeing the Mind

One of the most profound ways of truly experiencing the power of meditation is to spend two or three days just sitting, observing and experiencing the inner environment. Long periods of meditation can release the mind and the negativity that holds you prisoner in your own life.

Zen-style meditation is to sit, stay with every single outgoing breath, and allow all levels of the mind to reveal themselves. Unfortunately, at many prolonged meditation retreats there is often no warning, guidelines or preparation given in advance of what might potentially occur during the days ahead. Many people give up practising meditation completely because they find the experience so uncomfortable and emotionally disturbing.

Daily practice over an extended period of time can also have the same results. For no apparent reason, during a perfectly normal day a memory may suddenly flash into your mind, causing you to feel a kaleidoscope of unexpected emotions. The mind has been unlocked and released by the meditation practice. It is imperative at these times not to analyse, question or make judgements. Just sit and breathe evenly and deeply and really feel the emotions which are being presented.

The Journey into the Mind

Michael Rowland in his book *Absolute Happiness* gives one of the best explanations of the emotional layers through which we pass for final liberation of the mind. For a Western mind, particularly, this explanation is a 'route map' that lets us know that when these feelings arise it is all part of the process of releasing long-term negativity and pain which are being held trapped inside us, using up substantial amounts of valuable energy.

Rowland says that when we fully concentrate the mind over an extended period we may encounter six emotional layers:

- the personality
- boredom
- anger
- sadness
- fear
- love.

Rowland relates this explanation to Karma Yoga, which is the Yoga of concentration through action. The practice is to concentrate the mind and the breathing fully on simple daily activities, a philosophy similar to Zen Buddhist meditation practice, which instead of being physically active requires that we just sit and observe the mind. This is called *zazen*, which means 'sitting', and is considered to be the most essential practice for releasing the mind and attaining peace and sheer bliss. Concentration and single-minded focus of the mind, whether it be through physical action or meditative practices, is how we begin the journey towards liberating the mind from all its limiting and harmful constraints.

The breath is the thread that connects us to and brings integration and finally liberation from our painful experiences. It is imperative that with every feeling that reveals itself, whether pleasurable or painful, you follow with an outgoing breath. You observe – and when you have observed that you have become disconnected from the awareness of your breathing, you reconnect and continue being aware.

Know that these six emotional layers are a route map of sorts that actually won't make sense to anyone unless they begin a regular and dedicated practice of meditation.

The Personality

The Personality always has a shopping list of things to do, places to go, TV programmes to watch and people to see. It constantly chats away about current or immediate plans and concerns. It always has an opinion about who it is, what it wants, and who is right or wrong. To begin accessing the nature of the mind, this is the first layer that needs peeling back. In a three-day meditation retreat it can take almost the full day for this chatter to subside. With daily practice, a person can still remain on this layer for a very long time. The Personality is the hardest layer to penetrate because the world around us keeps feeding its wants and needs. Sitting in silence for even 10 minutes a day is enormously beneficial. Be aware that the mind can be most resistant, and when the chatter does begin to subside, *Boredom* is the next layer we must pass through.

Watch, observe, and keep breathing.

Boredom

Boredom is about avoidance. We avoid facing ourselves by keeping ourselves constantly busy and our minds forever occupied. The mind wants to be entertained and will do everything to avoid being busted on its nonsense and superfluous neediness. The personality will try and intervene and tell you that 'it's not working; this is a ridiculous exercise; there are too many things that need to be done rather than sitting here', etc., etc. This second layer desperately wants to keep the lid on what is below it, which is *Anger*.

Watch, observe, and keep breathing.

Anger

Long-term rage and resentment about the most trivial to the monumentally painful experiences can bubble to the surface. In this case Anger is definitely an emotion which is 'better out than in'. Lost pools of memory are stirred, which can be completely shocking and alarming to us. If we remember an adult or family member causing us harm or trauma, it is vital not to 'identify them and then crucify them as the cause of our pain'. To release these memories we must just feel and breathe and feel and breathe again. Integrate every single aspect of the memory and experiences felt at that time. As we process and experience anger, the next emotion to surface is *Sadness*.

Watch, observe, and keep breathing.

Sadness

Bursting into tears, despair, and the surfacing of memories which trigger feelings of deep regret or disappointment, can be so unnerving that we may think we are losing our grip on life as we know it, and may fear that we are precariously close to becoming seriously unbalanced and socially unacceptable. There is a story of a monk who was kneeling beside the grave of his recently departed master, crying. A man walking by stopped and said to him, 'Why are you crying?' The monk replied, 'Because I am sad.' This monk was honouring his feelings and expressing them accordingly. Our society as a whole does not give us permission to grieve or feel sadness. Don't analyse or question anything, just feel and breathe.

Watch, observe, and keep breathing.

Fear

The next emotion is *Fear*. The root of nearly all our limitations and physical and mental disharmonies is fear. At this stage of the meditation it is crucial that we remain connected to the breathing and focus on the image of an innocent child. Imagine how you would nurture this child through a terrifying nightmare. Imagine yourself being held, cuddled and reassured from within. Be the comforting adult to that frightened child – patient, understanding and immensely kind and gentle. The hardest fact for us all to grasp is that fear is an illusion. Most of us have great difficulty getting our heads around this one! Many programmes and documentaries have been dedicated to the subject of phobias. Fear of flying, spiders, snakes, water and public speaking have all been overcome when people have been slowly exposed to the actual subject of their fear. When their preconceived ideas and assumptions are slowly removed, there is no fear. It was an illusion. Many layers of fear grip all of us, preventing us from participating fully in life.

Fear can be a life-saving response when we are threatened with immediate danger. It is a most destructive and debilitating response when our whole lives function from it, preventing us from fully showing up in life. The fear we have to face in the end is fear of our own destruction. Figuratively speaking, it is like being in a dream in which you have to be willing to die. You have to be willing to give it all up and completely let go. When you finally give up, surrender yourself and completely let go; all the things from the past that held you prisoner and limited you dissolve. Only then can you be truly free.

Love

The final layer is *Love*. The only understanding most of us have of love in this Western world is through 'heartfelt' experiences. We fall in love, or love what we have or do. If any of these distinctive elements of our lives should suddenly change or be removed, we are devastated and plunged into despair and utter confusion. The mind or the alter-ego hates change, is judgemental, opinionated and only feels safe and happy under certain conditions and circumstances. If everything happens the way we think it should, then we love life and are happy. According to Eastern philosophy, this is a very superficial kind of love that is always short-lived and guarantees that we ride an emotional roller coaster throughout our lives. In all the ancient Eastern philosophies, love is described as an energy rather than an emotion. It is a deeply blissful, euphoric state of being which experiences all levels of reality devoid of judgement or opinion.

I believe that we can or are experiencing these six emotional layers all the time, but unconsciously. We can only change something when we become conscious of it or fully awake. I believe we can unconsciously pass through all six layers in an hour, in a 12-hour day, a month or over a period of months.

An example of this is the very first Yoga class I took shortly after arriving back in Australia in 1992. When Michael Rowland presented the six emotional layers at one of his Australian conferences, this memory immediately sprang to mind.

Having been advised to begin meditation and restorative Yoga as part of my Chronic Fatigue Syndrome recovery programme, I signed up for a class at one of Adelaide's Iyengar Yoga centres.

As the class began I remember thinking, 'This is easy. It's a bit like ballet. I am a good dancer. I can do this. I'd rather move my body, though, it's a bit stiff and static.' **The Personality** was in full flight.

As we continued making transitions from posture to posture, **Boredom** set in. I was bored with having to hold the postures for so long with not much else happening. I remember my breathing was choppy and irregular.

About halfway through the class the teacher asked us to go the wall for a headstand. She demonstrated the preparation, safety aspects and then how to take the legs up the wall for the upside-down position. I prepared, took on all the instructions, but could not lift my legs up the wall. I tried repeatedly to tip upside down and failed every time. I became filled with **Anger**. There was a lady in her fifties right next to me who was also having difficulty. I asked her seethingly, 'Can you do this?' She replied, 'Not yet', and continued calmly swinging her legs up until she was in her headstand posture. That was the last straw – someone older than me could do it and I couldn't! I sat with my back against the wall with my arms folded, furious and refusing to participate any further in this ridiculous exercise.

The teacher missed nothing! She asked us all to return to our mats and then in a very kind and gentle manner explained, 'Every Yoga posture has a purpose. Inversions, the headstand being one of them, chemically balances the brain and glands housed there through the increase of blood flow. It rests the inner organs and is a very beneficial posture for inner health. It is also about "tipping our world upside down". It will challenge any fears you have of change.' I had just returned to Australia having lost everything – my marriage, business, Golf GTi and very comfortable, entertaining lifestyle. I was utterly humiliated and shamed by my situation of having no money, no health and, after 17 years away, having to live with my parents. In the moments after the teacher's little explanation, **Sadness**, melancholy and overwhelming grief consumed me. I just wanted to sob and cry my heart out, and was teetering on the edge of leaving. Despite how overwhelmed I was feeling, I decided to stay.

Backbends were next on the agenda. **Fear** consumed me. I remember my whole body and mind feeling paralysed and completely resistant and unwilling even to try the preparations, let alone the full posture. The teacher kept reminding us to breathe. I sat on the floor and just breathed. I realize now how insightful and aware this teacher was. She left me alone and allowed me just to be with it all. Finally, I felt slightly calmer, watched the others and then took a deep breath and pushed upwards into Bow Pose. I was utterly amazed to find myself in the full posture, and was suddenly aware that the teacher was at my side. She supported the posture for me and allowed me to stay there comfortably, just breathing and experiencing the posture. Afterwards she told us, 'Backbends open up the heart area, an area we shut down through fear and emotional terror. Backbends can be most confronting postures. As you continue your practice of Yoga postures, what you experience and overcome in posture will also be reflected in your life. The physical transforms the metaphysical, influencing the mind, which transforms our lives.'

The class ended with Deep Relaxation in Corpse Pose. I remember at the end of the class being in an energetic state that I had never experienced before. I was completely calm, relaxed and peaceful. This, I imagine, must be fairly close to the sixth and final emotional layer: **Love**.

Being aware of how we may react emotionally to various situations and periods in our lives is a form of empowerment. Every experience is part of who we are, and we are our experiences.

The Role of the Breath in Meditation

'Never lose track of your breathing and you will never lose your way' is the most common advice given by teachers of Zen-style meditation. The key is always to remember that no matter what you experience as you meditate, if you follow the outgoing breath ceaselessly you will not 'fall out of your boat'. 'Staying in your boat' means to ride the waves of emotional experience from a detached place. As waves of disturbing memories come to the surface of your mind they may upset your breathing. Remain in your boat or on your seat of detached observation by following the breath; dare to let your consciousness flow no matter how painful or uncomfortable you may be feeling. Meditation frees the soul, your feelings, emotions and the lost parts of yourself. Know that your mind is the ocean of your whole life.

Making Meditation a Part of Your Life

'A journey of a thousand miles begins with a single step.'

Confucius

My recommendation is to prepare yourself slowly and gently with the first two stages of balancing the mind, breathing and deep relaxation. Begin practising stillness and surrender of the body first. Once you are comfortable with spending 10, 15, then 20 minutes of lying completely still in a deeply relaxed state, you are ready to move on to the practice of meditation. The following definitions may help you understand a little better the principles behind Zen-style meditation.

🕉 The Breath

Stay aware and experience your outgoing breath every time. Your breathing is like a wave: as you inhale, the wave swells and rises; as you exhale, the wave falls and descends.

🕉 Keep Your Seat

A comfortable posture: remaining aware of your outgoing breath, and awareness of riding the wave of every outgoing breath, is the meaning of 'keep your seat'.

🕉 Remembering

Remember to reconnect with your outgoing breath and keep your seat of awareness of the outgoing breath.

🕉 Discipline

Just do it. Sit daily, for a day or for two to three days consecutively.

Looking within and taking full responsibility for yourself takes great courage and determination. Releasing the negative emotions which have kept you contracted and imprisoned is the first step towards gaining control of your life and achieving a natural sense of balance and harmony. Meditation and Deep Relaxation can improve your ability to concentrate, become creative, decisive, to be fulfilled and content with your life. The key to this promised idyllic state is application of continuous patient, gentle practice.

The Chi Ball Method uses the principles of Zen-style meditation, which is just to sit with the eyes half or fully closed and focus on the breath, combined with movement to free stiffness from the body.

a typical chi ball class

The Development of the Chi Balls

The Chi Ball itself took three years of research and development. Colour, size, quality and the inclusion of various essential oils were tested and refined until the Chi Ball was versatile enough to cover every aspect of the concept.

Following consultation with exercise therapists in Australia, the most important factor was working how out the human spine should drape across the ball. The Chi Ball can be deflated or inflated by hand to cater for all levels of spinal flexibility. It is essential that the displacement of the Chi Ball material be at least 3 inches (7.5 centimetres) each side of a person's spinal column. Rolling the spine and pelvis around a hard surface is considered to be contraindicated or dangerous, especially if there are unknown conditions such as herniated or prolapsed discs.

Chi Ball Colours and Fragrances

The four colours used for the Chi Balls are orange, yellow, green and purple. These colours have been chosen for their energy and mood-enhancing qualities and for the fragrances with which they are associated. Your choice of colour can often also reveal your state of emotional or physical health.

Orange (Sweet Orange)

This Chi Ball colour is connected with happiness, joy, playfulness and spontaneity. Its sweet orange fragrance helps us to adopt an approach similar in tone. By releasing tension and frustration and moving stagnant chi, this aroma makes us feel more relaxed, confident and optimistic.

Yellow (Lemon Grass)

Self-esteem, ability, self-discipline and personal courage are connected with this Chi Ball colour, which can help lift us out of periods of self-doubt, fear and anxiety. Lemon grass aids this process by alleviating an overburdened mind and encouraging feelings of trust and confidence. It also clears the mind and enhances our ability to concentrate.

Green (Geranium)

Our capacity for compassion is connected with this Chi Ball colour and can therefore prevent us from indulging feelings of resentment, bitterness and cold-heartedness. To complement this, geranium enhances emotional sensitivity, helping us to feel stable, tranquil and secure.

Purple (Lavender)

The purple Chi Ball is associated with our desire for knowledge, our insight, intuition and how philosophical we tend to be. Lavender brings us out of a denial of any of these by releasing suppressed emotions, relieving feelings of anxiety or timidity, and calming our body and mind. We can attain a sense of physical peace using this fragrance.

The Five Components of a Chi Ball Class

Because of its links with the Five Elements and seasonal energy cycle, the content and format of a Chi Ball class changes throughout the year. But every class, no matter when it is performed, will use yin and yang to bring the body into balance.

A typical 90-minute class will generally follow this format:

1   Energize and Tone (including Tai Chi and Chi Kung), to generate heat and energy in preparation for Yoga

2   Yoga for strength, flexibility, determination, concentration and relaxation

3   Body Conditioning for balance, inner stabilization and strength

4   Feldenkrais, to develop flexibility and begin to allow the body to unwind

5   Deep Relaxation and Meditation, to calm both mind and body.

The exercises described in the more detailed explanation of a class, to follow, are just a selection of the moves I have adapted for Chi Ball. If you wish to practise yourself, begin slowly with one or two of the exercises from each section, which you can link into a mini-type class of your own.

You should always exercise according to how you feel, but as a very general rule Tai Chi or Chi Kung are best done during the morning as they help stimulate circulation. Perhaps to music you might try Energize and Tone (Chi Ball Aerobic Dance), then at midday, Yoga or Body Conditioning and Feldenkrais to revive flagging energy levels for the afternoon. Save Deep Relaxation for the evening, when you are getting ready for quietness and sleep.

However difficult you may find any of the exercises, or even just the discipline of making time for them, remember that perseverance does and will pay. Be patient with yourself, but also feel proud that you are helping to keep your body in good health.

Chi Ball Method: Energize and Tone

As discussed earlier, Energize and Tone has three exercise disciplines: Tai Chi, Chi Kung and Chi Ball Aerobic Dance. Each class may use one, two or all three elements of Energize and Tone to prepare and warm the body. Tai Chi is the bridge between Condensed Yin and Rising Yang. Consider Chi Kung as predominantly Rising Yang, and Chi Ball Aerobic Dance the link between Rising Yang and Radiant Yang.

Energize and Tone also reflects the Wood Element in our Five Elements theory, being executed slowly (Tai Chi) and with medium energy output (Chi Kung), building up to Fire (Chi Ball Aerobic Dance) as the moves become more energetic and we prepare for the Yoga section of the class.

Chi Ball Method: Tai Chi

We use aspects of Tai Chi to start a Chi Ball class in order to help focus the mind and engage greater use of the lungs. As the moves are simple and slow we can concentrate on detecting and releasing any tension and become aware of discrepancies in our breathing or balance; this is impossible to do when the exercise is fast. Although the exercises can be done in a more classical way without the use of a ball, it can help bring focus to those who find slow-moving exercise uncomfortable.

In Chi Ball we use eight moves that are specifically based on Tai Chi.

a

The Butterfly (TC1)

Stand with feet hip-width apart. As you slowly breathe in, raise your arms sideways to shoulder level, allowing the abdomen to swell slightly outwards.

As you breathe out, lower your arms, drawing the abdomen in towards the spine.

Swap the Chi Ball into the other hand and repeat on the other side.

Repeat 4 times each side.

As you raise the arms make sure the tips of the shoulders stay down. When lowering the arms, drop the elbows first, and allow the arms to float downwards.

Benefits

Gently stimulates breathing and relaxes neck, shoulders and upper back.

ASSOCIATED MERIDIAN

Lung

a

b

Push-the-Wind (TC2)

Stand with feet hip-width apart with the Chi Ball held at chest level.

Breathe in. As you breathe out, place the Chi Ball in your left hand and push it in front and across to the right side of the body. Twist from your navel centre first and then allow the shoulders to follow as you push the Chi Ball.

Breathe in to return the Chi Ball to the heart centre, facing the front and repeat to the other side. Keep the back straight, heart area raised and knees slightly bent.

Benefits

Releases tension in the upper back and shoulders. Stimulates spinal nerves, strengthens spinal muscles and increases blood flow to the brain.

ASSOCIATED MERIDIANS

Large and small intestines and the Triple Heater

a   b   c   d

Circle-the-Sun (TC3)

Stand with feet hip-width apart and hold the Chi Ball in both hands just below the heart area. As you breathe in, place the Chi Ball in the right hand and circle the arm across the body towards the left shoulder, above and behind the head.

Breathe out and open your arm out to the other side.

Finish with the Chi Ball held in front of the chest facing the front.

Benefits

Expands and stretches the waist and ribcage; releases stiffness and tension from the shoulders and upper back. The diaphragm is stretched and exercised, which helps improve breathing.

ASSOCIATED MERIDIANS

Heart and gallbladder

a   b   c

Circle-the-Moon (TC4)

Stand with feet hip-width apart and hold the Chi Ball in both hands just below the heart area. As you breathe in, place the Chi Ball in the right hand and open your arm out to the side, lean slightly back and draw a circle behind you with the Chi Ball across to the left shoulder.

Breathe out and pass the Chi Ball across the body; open arm out to the side.

Benefits

Opens and expands chest, releases stiffness and tension from shoulders, upper back, ribcage, waist. Improves breathing.

ASSOCIATED MERIDIANS

Lung, heart, gallbladder, large and small intestines

a

b

Scoop the Water (TC5)

Stand with feet hip-width apart. Breathe in and turn from the waist as you lift your right toe off the floor and pivot on the heel to open your body and leg slightly to the side.

Keep your right leg almost straight (knee soft) and, as you breathe out, bend over from the waist and trace the Chi Ball down along the thigh, knee, to the shin towards the ankle, keeping your shoulders back and down.

Breathe in, extend from the base of the spine and scoop the Chi Ball as you raise the body to a standing position.

Repeat 4 to 8 times on the right and then repeat to the left.

Benefits

Relieves stiffness from legs and hip muscles. Increases strength and flexibility in the spine.

ASSOCIATED MERIDIANS

Bladder and kidney

a b c

d e f

Energy Circle (TC6)

Begin with your feet together, Chi Ball held at navel area. Breathe in, place ball in right hand and open right arm and right leg with foot flexed to your imaginary right-hand corner.

Lunge forward and pass the Chi Ball behind your back.

Keep the left foot firmly planted into the ground as you breathe out and extend the arms out to the front.

Breathe in and transfer your weight back onto the left leg, bringing the Chi Ball to the chest.

Breathe out and turn the body to face the front.

Bring the feet back together.

Repeat to the left.

Benefits

Promotes circulation throughout the body. Stimulates breathing.

ASSOCIATED MERIDIANS

Lungs and small intestine

a   b   c

d   e   f

Scoop the Chi (TC7)

Begin with your feet together, Chi Ball held at navel area. Breathe in, place ball in right hand and open right arm and right leg with foot flexed to your imaginary right-hand corner.

Breathe out and lunge forward and reach for the Chi Ball in front of you, keeping the left foot firmly planted into the ground.

Breathe in, lunge back on to the left leg and draw a circle with the Chi Ball in your right hand towards an imaginary corner behind you.

Breathe out, lunge forward again and reach for the Chi Ball in front of you.

Breathe in, lunge back onto the left leg and draw a circle with the Chi Ball in your left hand towards the opposite imaginary corner behind you.

Breathe out, lunge forward and extend the arms out to the front.

Breathe in and transfer your weight back onto the left leg, Breathe out and face the front, bringing the feet together.

Benefits

Promotes circulation and effortless flow of breath with movement.

ASSOCIATED MERIDIANS

Lungs, pericardium, heart

a   b   c

The Wind (TC8)

Stand with feet hip-width apart.

Breathing in, lift the right elbow as high as possible without the shoulders lifting and tensing, and push the Chi Ball across the body to the right.

Breathe out, lift the left elbow as high as possible and push across to the left-hand side of the body.

Benefits

Improves mobility and flexibility of the ribcage.

ASSOCIATED MERIDIAN

Gallbladder

Chi Ball Method: Chi Kung

If you wish to develop your mind, pay attention to the body. If you wish to develop your spirit, pay attention to the mind.

Kenneth S. Cohen, *The Way of Qi Gong*

Aspects of Chi Kung's Eight Precious Exercises, mentioned earlier (page **37**) are used in Chi Ball to reawaken and encourage the circulation of chi throughout the body. In co-ordination with correct breathing (which should be through the nose) each exercise is repeated 8 times and must be done in a smooth and continuous manner either with the feet together (Neutral Stance) or the feet apart (Horse Stance).

a   b   c

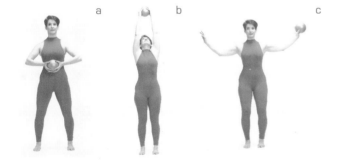

Rising Sun (CK1)

Stand in Horse Stance with feet hip-width apart. Breathe in and raise the Chi Ball to waist level.

Continue breathing in, pushing the Chi Ball above your head.

Breathe out and extend arms out to the side.

Repeat 8 times.

Benefits

Stretches and stimulates the Triple Heater meridian.

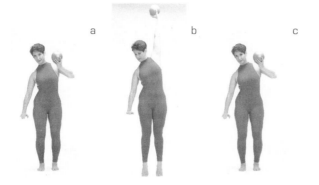

a   b   c

Press the Sky (CK2)

Stand in Horse Stance. Place the ball in the left hand. Breathe in and raise the Chi Ball to shoulder level.

Continue breathing in and extend your arm, pushing the Chi Ball skywards. Extend the right arm down, flexing the hand, and raise the heels off the floor.

Breathe out and lower your arm and Chi Ball down the front of the body.

Repeat 4 times on each side.

Benefits

Stretches and stimulates spleen, stomach, liver and gallbladder meridians.

a   b

Pulling the Bow (CK3)

Begin in Horse Stance with the Chi Ball in front of chest.

    Breathe in and extend your left arm to side and gently push Chi Ball away from the body as the right elbow is drawn back.

    Breathe out and lower the arms down.

    Repeat 4 times each side.

Benefits

Stretches and stimulates heart and lung meridians.

a   b

Twist and Look (CK4)

Begin in wide Horse Stance position, with the Chi Ball held at waist level.

    With the knees pressing out over the little toes, breathe in and twist your waist and shoulders to look behind.

    Breathe out and face the front.

    Repeat 4 times each side.

Benefits

Massages the inner organs, relieves stiffness in the neck and shoulders and stimulates the circulation of blood and chi.

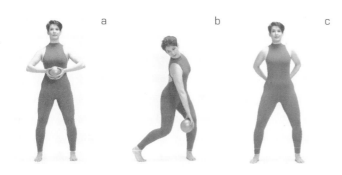

a   b   c

Twist and Release (CK5)

Begin in wide Horse Stance position, with ball held at waist level. Breathe in.

Breathe out and drop your right shoulder and right knee and swing the Chi Ball across the body down towards the floor.

Breathe in as you stand up and pass the Chi Ball behind your back.

Breathe out, drop the left shoulder and left knee and swing the Chi Ball across the body.

Repeat 8 times each side.

Benefits

Balances yin and yang energies, helps release anger and restores balance to the heart while improving breathing patterns.

a   b   c   d   e

Heaven and Earth (CK6)

Begin in wide Horse Stance position, with ball held at waist level. Breathe in as you raise the Chi Ball above head and slightly arch your upper back.

Breathe out and bend your knees to swing the Chi Ball through your legs, tucking your head under to look between them.

Breathe in to lift your head and extend the spine.

Continue breathing in to stand upright, passing the Chi Ball behind your back.

Repeat 8 times.

Benefits

Restores energy to the bladder, kidneys and adrenals, stimulates the meridians of the stomach and spleen. Promotes flexibility in the feet and legs.

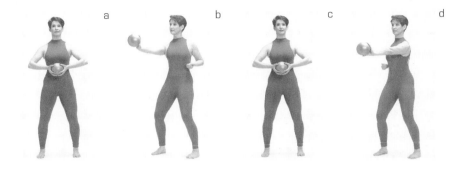

a   b   c   d

Energy Punch (CK7)

Begin in wide Horse Stance position, with ball held at waist level.

Breathe in to draw your left elbow back and your right hand (with Chi Ball) to punch forward.

Breathe in to draw ball back to waist.

Breathe out to draw right elbow back, punching forward with the left hand (with Chi Ball).

Repeat 4 times on each side.

Benefits

Stimulates, energizes and eliminates toxins from the liver. Promotes circulation of blood and chi.

a

b

Energy Bounce (CK8)

Begin with feet in narrow Horse Stance position, with the Chi Ball held in your right hand. Breathe in and raise up onto your toes, swinging your arms to catch the Chi Ball in front.

Breathe out, dropping with a slight 'bounce' down into the heels, swinging the Chi Ball backwards in left hand.

Repeat 16 times.

Benefits

Stimulates all meridian points in the feet, energizes the central nervous system, strengthens the skeletal system and improves the circulation.

Chi Ball Method: Chi Ball Aerobic Dance

To practise Chi Ball Aerobic Dance, pick one or two moves and repeat 16 to 32 times. Once you become familiar with each movement, try joining three or four together to form a sequence. Make sure you also incorporate the principles of posture, rhythm and flow, space and breathing, as discussed in Chapter 2.

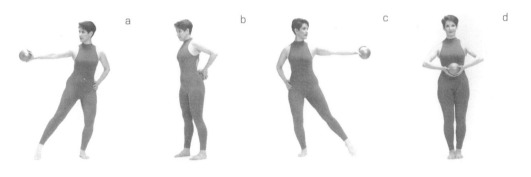

a   b   c   d

Around-the-World (CB1)

Stand with feet together with the Chi Ball held at waist level. Breathe in and extend the right arm and leg and step out to the side.

Continue breathing in as you bring your feet together and pass the Chi Ball behind your back to the left hand.

Breathe out as you step onto your right leg again, extending the left arm and leg to the side, then bringing the feet together again.

Repeat 4 to 8 times each side, making wider and wider circles around the body each time. Explore the space around your body!

Benefits

Expands chest area for improved breathing.

a

b

Ocean Wave (CB2)

Stand in wide Horse Stance position and place the Chi Ball in the right hand. Breathe in and wave your arm across your body.

Breathe out and open your arm away from your body in a generous sweeping movement.

Repeat this movement 8 to 16 times. Be adventurous: use different shapes and lines each time, as you explore the space around you. Allow your body to respond naturally and intuitively to each sweeping movement your arm chooses to make.

Swap sides.

Benefits

Releases tension and stiffness in shoulders, upper back and ribcage. Circulation increases to muscles in the arms and legs, as heart rate increases and body temperature rises.

ASSOCIATED MERIDIANS

Triple Heater, large and small intestines

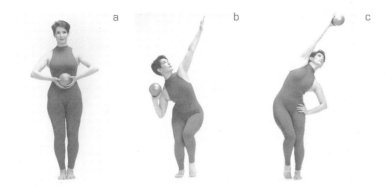

a   b   c

Lightning (CB3)

Stand with feet together with the Chi Ball at waist level and breathe in. Place the Chi Ball in the right hand and step sideways to the right into a deep squat, with your feet together as you breathe out.

Breathe in as you step sideways to the left, pushing the Chi Ball up and over, allowing the body to bend gently to the side.

Move slowly and smoothly and repeat 4 to 8 times each side.

Benefits

Stretches waist and ribcage. Strengthens and tones thigh and buttock muscles.

ASSOCIATED MERIDIAN

Gallbladder

a   b   c

Rainbow (CB4)

Begin with your feet together with the Chi Ball held in both hands on the left side of your body.

Breathe in as you step out sideways to the right, tracing the imaginary shape of a rainbow over your head with the Chi Ball in your right hand.

Breathe out and bring your feet together to the other side of your body, catching the Chi Ball with your left hand.

Repeat 8 to 16 times side to side.

Benefits

Mobilizes upper back muscles and shoulders, stretches waist and ribcage, stimulates circulation of blood and chi.

ASSOCIATED MERIDIAN

Gallbladder

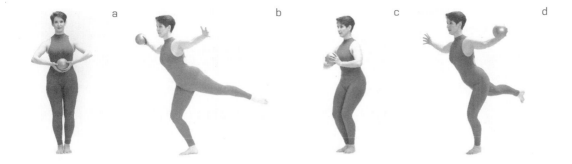

a   b   c   d

The Swallow (CB5)

Begin with feet together with the Chi Ball held at waist level.

Breathe in as you step forward onto your right leg, and with the Chi Ball in your right hand sweep the arms forward and out to the side in a generous, expansive motion, as if you were attempting to fly like a swallow. Make sure you bend deeply onto the right leg and extend the left leg away from the body behind you. Elevate the heart area and lengthen the front of the body.

Breathe out as you take two steps backwards and then breathe in again as you step onto your left leg.

Repeat 4 to 8 times on each leg.

Benefits

Releases pent-up energy and frustration and overall physical stress and tension. Promotes the expression of joy, enthusiasm and confidence as the heart and chest area is expanded and stretched.

ASSOCIATED MERIDIANS

Lung, large intestine, conception vessel

The Storm (CB6)

Begin with your feet together with the Chi Ball in your right hand. Breathe in and drop your right arm and shoulder forward.

> Breathe out as you scoop the Chi Ball overhead and out to the right side of the body.
>
> Keep the motion fluid, soft and springy to protect the knees.
>
> Repeat 4 to 8 times on each side.

Benefits

Tones thighs and buttocks, releases stiffness and tension in the neck, shoulders, ribcage and lower back muscles.

ASSOCIATED MERIDIANS

Stomach, spleen, liver, gallbladder

a   b   c   d

Sunset (CB7)

Begin with both feet together, Chi Ball held at waist level. Breathe in and step with the right foot sideways, extending your right arm and Chi Ball with the leg.

Breathe out as you cross the left foot behind the right, squatting down into a deep curtsey.

If you have knee problems, use the alternative squat (picture d).

Repeat 4 to 8 times on each side.

Benefits

Improves flexibility in ankles and hips. Strengthens and tones thigh, buttock and postural back muscles.

ASSOCIATED MERIDIANS

Bladder, lung, pericardium, Triple Heater

a   b   c   d

Sunrise (CB8)

Begin with your feet together in a deep squat, with the Chi Ball held at chest level. Either with feet remaining together or with your left foot tucked behind, breathe in as you push the Chi Ball towards the ceiling, stretching the whole body.

Breathe out as you squat down into a deep curtsey.

If you have knee problems, avoid bending deeply and use the alternative steps, c and d.

Repeat 4 to 8 times, taking a full breath in as you extend up, and a full breath out as you squat.

Benefits

Stretches entire body and is beneficial for the heart, diaphragm (improving circulation to abdominal area, helping digestive problems), lungs and entire spine (relieves backache and neck problems).

ASSOCIATED MERIDIANS

Lung, heart, Triple Heater, bladder

a   b   c

Half-Moon (CB9)

Begin with the Chi Ball held in front of body and feet wide apart.

Breathe in as you scoop the Chi Ball down and across to the right side of the body, as if swinging a golf club.

Continue breathing in as you scoop across to the left side.

Breathe out as you again scoop to the right and left.

Repeat – 2 swings to breathe in and 2 swings to breathe out – 8 times.

Benefits

Brings flexibility and tone to the hips, waist, middle and lower back muscles. Relieves lower back pain. Stimulates liver organ when twisting across to the right and stomach/spleen organs when twisting left. Twisting the waist helps balance the yin and yang energies and calms the heart.

ASSOCIATED MERIDIANS

Pericardium, Triple Heater

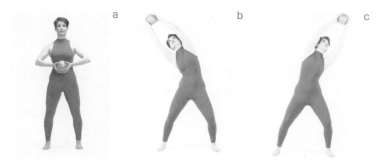

a   b   c

Full Moon (CB10)

Begin with the Chi Ball held in front of your body and feet wide apart.

Breathe in as you keep the Chi Ball in both hands, scooping it across to the right, passing the Chi Ball over your head as you breathe out, tracing in the air a large, spacious circle up and over the body to the left.

Repeat 4 to 8 times each side.

Benefits

Fully stretches the waist, all the spinal muscles and diaphragm; balances the skeletal system. Breathing in and raising the arms overhead increases lung volume. Breathing out expels waste energy, relieving lethargy and fatigue.

ASSOCIATED MERIDIANS

Large intestine, liver, gallbladder

Chi Ball Method: Yoga

Yoga reflects the Fire Element and Radiant Yang of the energy cycle. The sequences of standing or seated postures, linked together in a fluid way with moving choreography, build heat, fire and passion. We focus in this section on developing strength, stability and flexibility without tension, and on clearing our minds as well as our bodies of unwanted debris. We would use between 6 and 10 Yoga postures in a typical Chi Ball class, depending on the time of year.

a b c d

Mountain Pose (*Tadasana*) (Y1)

Begin with your feet together and parallel with your toes spread evenly, holding the Chi Ball in both hands.

Draw your inner ankles up, lifting the arches of the feet. Activate your legs without locking the knees by drawing your thigh muscles up towards your hips. Draw your navel in and up, very slightly dropping the tail bone down and lifting the pubic bone. Roll your shoulders back and down and feel the shoulder blades moving down towards the hips. Allow the skin on the back of the body also to soften and melt downwards towards the hips. Draw your chin into the throat without over-extending the neck vertebrae. Be conscious of pushing down into the feet and lengthening the spine upwards.

Transfer the Chi Ball into your right hand as you breathe in and raise your arms out to the side.

Continue breathing in as you raise the Chi Ball overhead.

Attempt to push the Chi Ball up into the ceiling to create space inside the body. Swap the ball into your left hand as you breathe out, and lower your arms.

Repeat 6 to 8 times, swapping the Chi Ball at the top of the pose from the right to the left sides.

Benefits

Establishes a firm postural base and builds awareness; establishes correct alignment for all poses; this correct alignment allows 'space' for inner organs, aiding digestion; frees the diaphragm and improves breathing.

a   b   c   d

Difficult Pose (*Uttkatasana*) (Y2)

Begin in Mountain Pose. Draw your navel to your spine, lengthen your tail bone down towards heels. Rotate shoulders back and down, and allow the shoulder blades to slide down towards your hips. Place the Chi Ball in your right hand; breathe in as you stretch your arms out to the side.

Continue breathing in until the Chi Ball is overhead in both hands.

Breathe out and bend your knees into a deep squat, keeping chest high, by lifting the heart area and opening the armpits.

Keep the breath smooth and even, and relax your facial muscles. Breathe in and press down into your heels to straighten your legs. Breathe out as you transfer the Chi Ball into the left hand, lowering the arms down to the side.

WARNING

If you have high blood pressure, please avoid raising your arms above your head. Use the option illustrated right instead.

Benefits

Relieves shoulder tension; strengthens lower back muscles; strengthens ankle joints; promotes even development of leg muscles; strengthens chest muscles, lifts diaphragm and provides gentle massage to the heart; firms abdominal muscles.

a b

Tree Pose (*Vrkasana*) (Y3)

Begin with your feet together in Mountain Pose.

Breathe in as you transfer your weight onto your right leg, with your feet parallel and toes spread for a firm foundation. Place the sole of your left foot as high on your inner right thigh as possible. (If you have difficulty balancing, use a chair or wall for support.) Breathe out to stabilize the posture, pressing your left knee back, your left foot into the right thigh and right thigh pushing against your left foot. This two-way pressure helps keep the leg and foot in place. Drop your tail bone down towards your heels. Lift the heart and open the chest by rolling your shoulders back and down and allow the shoulder blades to slide towards your hips. Breathe in as you push the Chi Ball above your head. Remain there, concentrating on balance for 3 to 5 full breaths.

Remain calm and steady in both your mind and body. Keep your eyes fixed on a point in front of you. Allowing your eyes to flicker and the mind to wander affects your ability to balance.

WARNING

If you have high blood pressure, please avoid raising your arms above your head. Use the alternative pose illustrated right instead.

Benefits

Improves concentration, balance, confidence and poise; strengthens joints and muscles of legs and feet; increases flexibility in ankles, knees and hips; opens the chest and relieves shoulder and upper back tension.

a   b   c

Triangle Pose (*Trikonasana*) (Y4)

Begin with your feet together in Mountain Pose. Breathe in as you step the feet and legs wide apart (about 3½feet/1 metre) with toes facing forward. Breathe out and wait.

Breathe in; turn your right foot out to a 90-degree angle and your left foot in by about 20 degrees (your right foot should be in line with the arch of your left foot). Breathe out and wait. Try and keep your hips facing front even though your feet have been turned to the side.

Draw up your thigh muscles to activate the whole leg. Draw your navel up and back into the spine. Press your shoulders down as you float your arms up to shoulder height with the Chi Ball in your left hand.

Breathe out; look along your right arm as you tip your body sideways to clasp either your right shin or ankle, allowing the left arm and hand to float up vertically.

Hold for 3 to 5 breaths. As you breathe out, roll the left hip back and draw the right buttock forward. Lengthen your spine from your tail bone to the crown of your head. Breathe in to raise your body. Breathe out to turn the feet parallel. Repeat to the left side.

Benefits

Improves postural alignment; stretches hips, back and legs; strengthens neck muscles and ankle joints; improves lateral stretch of spine; stretches and stimulates spinal nerves; improves digestion.

a   b   c

Extended Side Angle Posture (*Utthita Parsvakonasana*) (Y5)

Begin with your feet together in Mountain Pose. Breathe in as you step the feet and legs wide apart (about 4 1/2 feet/1.2 metres) with toes facing forward. Breathe out and wait. Breathe in; turn your right foot out to a 90-degree angle and your left foot in by about 20 degrees (your right foot should be in line with the arch of your left foot). Breathe out and wait. Try and keep your hips facing front even though your feet have been turned to the side. Draw up your thigh muscles to activate the whole leg. Draw your navel up and back into the spine. Press your shoulders down as you float your arms up to shoulder height with the Chi Ball in your left hand.

Breathe in as you lengthen your spine and waist; breathe out as you bend your right knee, rolling the left hip back and making sure that the right knee is tracking over the centre of your right foot.

Breathe in, then breathe out as you place the fingertips of your right hand on the big-toe side of the foot; extend your left arm over head.

Turn head and look under your left armpit to the ceiling.

NOTE

Work with the modified pose first if you feel this stretch is too advanced (see picture c). Breathe in to raise your body, breathe out to turn the feet parallel. Repeat to the left side.

Benefits

Increases strength and flexibility of ankles, knees, thighs, hips and back; opens chest, stretches ribcage, frees diaphragm; relieves sciatica and arthritic pains; strengthens shoulders and reduces tension. Excellent for digestive and eliminative systems (stimulates the liver when you lean to the right, the stomach and spleen when you lean to the left).

Warrior 1 (*Virarbhadrasana* 1) [Y6]

Begin with your feet together in Mountain Pose. Breathe in as you step the feet and legs wide apart (about 4½ feet/1.2 metres) with toes facing forward. Breathe out and wait. Breathe in; turn your right foot out to a 90-degree angle and your left foot in by about 20 degrees (your right foot should be in line with the arch of your left foot). Breathe out and wait. Try and keep your hips facing front even though your feet have been turned to the side. Draw up your thigh muscles to activate the whole leg. Draw your navel up and back into spine. Press your shoulders down as you float your arms up to shoulder height with the Chi Ball in your left hand.

Breathe in as you lengthen your spine and waist; breathe out as you bend your right knee, rolling the left hip back and making sure that the right knee is tracking over the centre of your right foot.

Straighten your left leg and extend the torso up. Keep your feet flat on floor and distribute your weight through both legs. Feel a full extension from the Chi Ball in the left hand across your chest to the fingers of your right hand. Breathe in to raise your body. Breathe out to turn the feet parallel. Repeat to the left side.

Benefits

Stretches and opens the hip joints, pelvic floor and inner thigh muscles; strengthens all leg muscles, buttocks and arches of the feet; increases elasticity and strength of the spine and back muscles; strengthens the abdominal, shoulder and arm muscles; strengthens intention and determination.

Warrior 2 (*Virarbhadrasana* 2) (Y7)

Begin with your feet together in Mountain Pose. Breathe in as you step the feet and legs wide apart (about 4½ feet/1.2 metres) with toes facing forward. Breathe out and wait.

Hold your Chi Ball at chest level. Breathe in as you lift your right heel and bend the right leg. Breathe out and turn your hips to face the right foot. Turn your left foot in 60 degrees and right foot out 90 degrees, keeping the left leg extended and your hips level.

Breathe in, then breathe out as you bend your right knee. Breathe in and push the Chi Ball straight up towards the ceiling, and breathe out as you either look up at the ball (as shown) or straight ahead.

Hold this pose for 3 to 5 breaths. Drop the shoulders down and allow the skin on the back of your body to soften and slide downwards. Breathe in, breathe out to turn body back to the front and the feet parallel. Repeat to the left side.

WARNING

If you have high blood pressure, please avoid raising your arms above your head. Keep the Chi Ball held to your chest instead (see step c).

Benefits

Opens chest, increases lung capacity and improves deep breathing; develops physical stamina throughout the body; increases energy and stimulates the central nervous system; strengthens leg muscles, back and arms; relieves stiffness in shoulders, neck and back.

 a

 b

 c

Reverse Triangle Pose (*Parivrtta Trikonasana*) (Y8)

Prepare as for Warrior 2 but with your feet 3 feet (1 metre) apart instead, and turning to face your right foot.

Turn your left foot in 60 degrees and right foot out 90 degrees, keeping your hips level. Breathe in then breathe out to bend your right knee, keeping your left leg straight with the heel slightly raised. Spiral round until your chest is facing the back wall; breathe in as you lengthen the waist, breathe out as you place your left elbow on your right knee, allowing the right arm and hand to float up vertically.

If this posture is a little too challenging, do the standing twist (step c) instead, as shown.

Benefits

Strengthens back muscles (due to increased blood supply), hips, thighs, calves and hamstrings; expands the chest and improves breathing; tones and massages abdominal organs; releases tension and pain in the back; improves balance, concentration and determination.

Pyramid (*Parsvottanasana*) (Y9)

Begin with your feet together in Mountain Pose. Breathe in as you step the feet and legs wide apart (about 4$\frac{1}{2}$feet/1.2 metres) with toes facing forward. Breathe out and wait.

Hold your Chi Ball at chest level. Breathe in as you lift your left heel and bend the left leg. Breathe out to turn your hips to face the right foot. Turn your left foot in 60 degrees and right foot out 90 degrees. Draw up your thigh muscles to activate both legs and keep your hips level. Press down evenly into both feet.

Breathe in to place both hands on the Chi Ball behind your back, moving the elbows towards each other. Extend your torso forward at a 45-degree angle away from the pelvis and out and over the right leg. Lift the heart to open the chest and slide the shoulder blades down your back, towards your waist.

Once again, if this pose is too challenging, practise the supported pyramid posture (step b) instead. Breathe in to raise your body. Breathe out to turn the feet parallel. Repeat to the left side.

Benefits

Excellent leg, back and shoulder stretch; increases flexibility of hips, spine, shoulders and legs; strengthens the legs; tones abdominal organs; develops balance and stamina and improves circulation throughout the body and head.

a   b

Pose of a Dancer (*Natarajasana*) (Y10)

Begin with your feet together in Mountain Pose.

Breathe in as you transfer your weight onto your right leg, with your feet parallel and toes spread for a firm foundation. Bend your left knee and clasp either the foot or ankle from behind, drawing the knee slightly behind the standing leg. (If you have difficulty balancing, use a chair or wall for support.) Breathe out to stabilize the posture.

Drop your tail bone down towards your heels. Lift the heart to open the chest, roll your shoulders back and down and allow the shoulder blades to slide towards your waist and move the elbow back.

Breathe in as you push the Chi Ball above your head. Breathe out and remain there, concentrating on balance for 3 to 5 full breaths.

Stay calm and steady in both your mind and body. Keep the eyes fixed on a point in front of you. Allowing your eyes to flicker and the mind to wander affects your ability to balance.

Repeat on the other leg.

Benefits

Strengthens joints and firms muscles of the leg, back and chest; tones and calms the central nervous system; stretches the upper body, front of hip and thigh muscles; improves physical and mental balance and poise.

Staff Pose (*Dandasana*) (Y11)

Place the Chi Ball between your ankles and then sit with your back straight and legs extended. Turn up your toes and gently press the backs of your knees towards the floor. Press your hands into the floor alongside hips. Breathe in: draw navel in, lengthen waist, lift chest and heart and stretch collarbones away from each other. Breathe out: draw shoulders back and down, pressing down into hands to achieve more lift in the posture.

Hold this posture for 3 to 5 breaths.

If you have difficulty sitting up straight, try sitting on the edge of a folded blanket to lift the pelvis.

Benefits

Brings relief to gastric complaints; tones the kidneys; trains the lower back for strength and for forward bends; straightens spine; releases lower back tension and encourages full deep breathing.

Seated Forward Fold (*Paschimottanasana*) (Y12)

Begin in Staff Pose with the Chi Ball between your ankles. Breathe in, breathe out: draw your navel into spine and extend forward over your legs. Try and extend the spine, making space between each disc before folding over your legs. Keep your legs 'alive' by gently drawing up the thigh muscles.

Lengthen through the crown of your head and heels of your extended legs. Remain in this pose for 3 to 5 breaths.

Breathe in to extend the body up, breathe out to fully release.

If your legs are very stiff, try one of the three alternative modifications shown below.

Benefits

Massages, stimulates and prevents sluggishness in the abdominal organs; rejuvenates the whole spine and improves digestion; extended periods spent stretching in this posture improve the oxygenated blood supply to the pelvic area and reproductive organs, which increases vitality and helps cure impotency.

Head to Knee (*Janu Sirasana*) (Y13)

Sit in Staff Pose, drawing the sole of your right foot to the inner side of your left thigh. Place the Chi Ball underneath the right thigh, knee or shin (the position will depend on your hip flexibility), and allow the knee to relax down onto the Chi Ball. Make sure the hips are in a straight line, not one hip twisted back.

Breathe in: lengthen body and also turn the body towards your left leg. Breathe out: relax shoulders down and draw your navel back into your spine as you begin folding forward from the hips and base of your spine over the extended leg.

Keep your leg 'alive' by gently drawing up the thigh muscles. Lengthen through the crown of your head and heel of your extended leg. Remain in the pose for 3 to 5 breaths. Breathe in to extend the body up, breathe out to fully release. Repeat with the other leg.

If you find this difficult, try one of the two alternative modifications shown.

Benefits

Strengthens and elongates the spine; excellent leg stretch; relieves lower back tension and opens hips, knees and ankles; stimulates and improves circulation through spine, torso and abdominal organs; improves digestion and elimination; calms and settles the mind.

a   b

Cobra (*Bhujangasana*) (Y14)

Lie face down with the Chi Ball placed on the breast bone and your hands beneath your shoulders. Breathe in: extend your chest out and along the Chi Ball as if you are trying to push it away from you with your chest. Breathe out: hold the posture. Continue holding for 3 to 5 breaths.

This action elongates the spine and avoids the risk of adding undue pressure to the spinal discs. Avoid pressing down into the hands, encouraging the back to lengthen and strengthen under its own weight. Draw the elbow in towards the side of the body, drawing your shoulders away from your ears and sliding the shoulder blades down the back.

Benefits

Improves intervertebral strength and flexibility of the spine; full front of body stretch for legs, abdomen, chest and throat; stimulates circulation to muscles and nerves; improves digestion and relieves constipation; relieves menstrual disorders and rejuvenates reproductive organs.

a   b   c   d

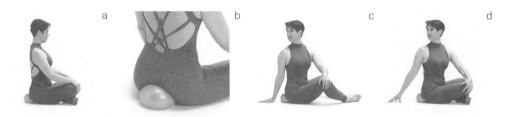

Spinal Twist (*Matsyendrasana*) (Y15)

Sit cross-legged on the floor, half sitting on the Chi Ball as shown.

Elongate the spine and draw the chin into the throat. Breathe in: lengthen your spine and waist further. Breathe out: place the heel of your right hand at the base of your spine about 5 inches (12 centimetres) away from your buttocks. Turn from the navel to twist the abdomen, ribs, chest, shoulders and lastly the neck, to look over your right shoulder. Remain in the twist for 3 to 5 breaths.

Imagine your spine sliding up a pole as you breathe, and then spiralling around the pole as you breathe out. Breathe in, then breathe out to release the twist and return to the front. Repeat on the other side.

Benefits

Strengthens the back and rotates spine fully; relieves backache caused by muscular tension; stretches hips; massages liver, spleen and intestines; frees chest and promotes elasticity in shoulders.

a   b

Bridge Pose (*Setu Bandha Sarvangasana*) (Y16)

Lie down on your back, knees bent and feet hip-width apart, parallel and flat on the floor close to your buttocks. Place your arms beside your body, palms down. Roll to one side and place the Chi Ball between your shoulder blades, then clasp your hands behind your head and slowly arch your spine over the ball, carrying your head to the floor. Remove your hands and either raise them above your head or place them beside your body.

Breathe in: slowly raise your hips off the floor until the line from your shoulders to your knees is at a 45-degree angle.

Breathe out: push down into your feet and gently slide your shoulders towards your hips. The Chi Ball is there to support the centre of your back to make it easier to elongate the lower spine and elevate the pelvis. Allow the tail bone to move slightly forward and the pubic bone to tilt towards the navel. Continue to breathe in; feel your body lift slightly off the Chi Ball and the weight of the upper body relax down again as you breathe out.

Benefits

Strengthens lower back, gluteals, abdominals, neck and shoulders; improves flexibility of whole spinal column; nourishes spinal nerves; the pressure of the chin against the chest massages the thyroid gland and aids regulation of metabolism; massages heart and lungs through deep abdominal breathing; helps cure insomnia and depression; relieves fatigue.

a   b

Supported Fish Pose (*Arda Marsyasana*) (Y17)

Lie down on your back, legs straight and feet flexed with ankles together. Roll to one side and place the Chi Ball between your shoulder blades, then clasp your hands behind your head and slowly arch your spine over the ball, carrying your head to the floor. Place your hands on the side of your hips. Breathe in: press down into the elbows to arch your neck, tipping your head backwards. Elevate your chest until the crown of your head comes onto the floor. Breathe out: draw your shoulder blades down towards the hips.

Continue to breathe in and feel your chest and throat open, the body lift slightly off the Chi Ball and the feet stretch away from you. Breathe out: try and sustain the feeling of length in the body and the lift and openness of the chest.

NOTE

For severe neck problems, please use the alternative Supported Fish Pose, placing the Chi Ball under the neck as shown in step b.

Benefits

Increases blood circulation and flexibility in shoulders, thoracic and lumbar spine; improves lung capacity and stimulates the parathyroid; with the crown of the head on the floor the pituitary and pineal glands benefit; soothes emotions and mental stress; relieves energy blocks in the spleen, stomach and lung meridians.

Supine Abdominal Twist (*Jathara Parivartanasana*) (Y18)

Begin by lying down on your back, feet on the floor, knees bent and arms stretched sideways. Place the Chi Ball between your knees. Breathe in: shift your hips about 5 inches (12 centimetres) to the right. Breathe out: bend the knees over your abdomen.

Breathe in: simultaneously press the right shoulder down and extend the right arm away from the body. Breathe out: lower the knees to the left side onto the floor.

Breathe in: turn your head to look along your right arm. Breathe out: press the right shoulder down and revolve the ribcage and abdomen towards the right, keeping the hips stable. Remain for 3 to 5 breaths.

Breathe in, then breathe out to raise the knees over the abdomen and replace the feet on the floor.

Repeat to the other side.

Benefits

Eradicates energy blocks in the liver, spleen/pancreas and stomach; strengthens abdominal muscles and cures digestive irregularities; relieves general aches and pains in the lower back and hip area.

Corpse Pose (*Shavasana*) (Y21)

Sit with knees bent, holding the backs of the knees, and roll backwards slowly, lowering the spine, neck and head to the floor. Extend the legs and feet and allow them to drop apart evenly sideways. Place the arms beside the body, palms up.

On each breath let the body melt into the floor. Widen the collarbones, open the ribcage, move the chest away from the abdomen. Keep the abdomen soft and relaxed. Bring your attention to your breathing and gradually relax one muscle at a time when you breathe out. Remain in this pose for 5 to 10 minutes.

Benefits

Allows time for the body to integrate what has been experienced, challenged and learned through the postures; encourages relaxation in the muscles; nourishes the nervous system and internal organs and calms the mind.

Chi Ball Method: Body Conditioning

The nature of the Body Conditioning exercises reflect the Earth Element and Descending Yang, in which we begin to cool down from the fiery aspects of Yoga to stabilize the body and consolidate chi.

In the Chi Ball Method I have adapted Joseph Pilates' moves in such a way that we get the benefits without the frustrations that many trying pure Pilates® for the first time often experience. Using the ball as a focal point, Chi Ball participants are able more quickly to grasp the concept and gain an understanding, early on, of what it is to feel balanced, stable, centrally strong and aware of their posture.

Most of the moves take place on the floor which, far from popular belief, can – when done with grace, power and co-ordination – provide as great a challenge as any exercise done while standing. Improvements in muscle tone, body shape and co-ordination are equally as profound.

Body Conditioning is used in the Chi Ball Method to consolidate chi by developing our core strength and stability. Focus is forced inwards as performing these moves requires concentration, co-ordination and breath control. Discipline and repetition of the moves brings skill, grace and effortless execution of the various exercises.

For some pointers before you begin, see pages **47–57**.

a   b   c

Warm-up: Neck Extension (BC1)

Lie down on your back, knees bent and feet hip-width apart, parallel, flat and a comfortable distance from your buttocks. Place the Chi Ball at the top of the neck and base of the head.

    Breathe in: arch your neck over the Chi Ball.

    Breathe out and draw the chin into the throat and feel the neck elongate.

    Repeat this 8 to 10 times without exerting too much effort.

Benefits

Relieves neck tension.

a   b

Warm-up: Scapular Awareness (BC2)

Lie down on your back, with knees bent and feet hip-width apart, parallel, flat and a comfortable distance from your buttocks. Place your arms beside your body with the Chi Ball underneath your right hand.

Breathe in and breathe out as you gently push the Chi Ball towards your right foot. Become aware of the action and feeling of the shoulder joint and shoulder blades sliding along the floor towards the hips.

Breathe in to release; breathe out to push the Chi Ball towards your foot.

Benefits

Relieves stiffness and tension in the shoulders.

a   b   c

Warm-up: Pelvic Tilt (BC3)

Lie down on your back, with knees bent and feet hip-width apart, parallel, flat and a comfortable distance from your buttocks. Raise your pelvis and place the Chi Ball at the base of your spine – just below the low back and top of the sacrum. Place your arms beside your body, palms down or raise them above your head.

Breathe in, then breathe out to push gently with the feet to drop the waist towards the floor, flattening the back against the Chi Ball, pushing the pubic bone up.

Breathe in to arch your back over the Chi Ball.

Be careful not to over-exaggerate this movement. A gentle tilt back and forth over the Chi Ball is all that is required to awaken pelvic movement.

Benefits

Mobilizes and opens lower back.

Spinal Roll (BC4)

Part 1: Lie down on your back, knees bent and feet hip-width apart, parallel, flat and a comfortable distance from your buttocks. Place the Chi Ball between your knees and your hands behind your head.

Breathe in and, as you breathe out, simultaneously press the left shoulder down and roll your knees sideways towards the floor. Allow the left foot to lift off the floor so that the knees stay in alignment with each other.

Breathe in, then breathe out as you press your left shoulder into the floor and navel into the spine, hollowing the abdomen to bring the knees back to centre. Repeat to the left side.

Execute the whole sequence 6 to 8 times.

NOTE

If your shoulder is lifting off the floor you have executed the exercise beyond your range of motion. Make sure the shoulders remain firmly pressed against the floor throughout the movement.

d e f

Part 2: Now raise your knees over the hips. Roll to the right and left again. Keep your knees aligned.

Repeat this sequence 6 to 8 times with the same breathing pattern as before.

Benefits

Strengthens oblique muscles, to support the spine; strengthens and tones waist; mobilizes lower back and hips.

a   b   c

d

Foot Paddle (BC 5)

Lie down on your back, knees bent and feet hip-width apart, parallel, flat and a comfortable distance from your buttocks. Raise your pelvis and place the Chi Ball at the base of your spine – just below the low back and top of the sacrum. Make sure your hips are even and the pubic bone is level (neither tilted up or down).

Place your arms beside your body, palms down. Breathe in to lengthen your neck and raise your arms over your head, breathe out to lift your right foot 2 inches (5 centimetres) off the floor.

Breathe in, then breathe out to raise both arms towards the ceiling.

Breathe in, then breathe out to lengthen your right leg.

Continue keeping the neck long, your hips level and the shoulders gently pressed into the floor and sliding towards your hips. Breathe in to bend your knee and return your arms above your shoulders. Breathe out to lower your arms and foot to the floor.

Benefits

Trains postural muscles to help stabilize the spine for daily activities; retrains essential postural stabilizing muscles following episodes of back pain or injury.

a   b

Shoulder Bridge 1 (BC6)

Lie on your back with the Chi Ball positioned underneath your pelvis – at the base of the spine (not in the lower back). Very subtly lift your pubic bone to make sure it is level with your navel (avoid flattening the lower back or dropping your waist). Make sure your hips are even.

Either keep your hands by your side or raise your arms above your head. Keep your shoulders moving down towards your hips, keep the base of the ribcage in and moving down towards your hips. Breathe in, breathe out, flatten your navel to your spine and, leading with your pubic bone, lift your pelvis off the ball, with your shoulders to knees in a straight 45-degree angle to the floor. Take three full breaths in this position, keeping the waist stretched and long.

Breathe in, breathe out to lower yourself back down onto the Chi Ball. Repeat twice more.

Benefits

Tones buttocks, back of legs (hamstrings), strengthens whole spinal column and postural support muscles. Abdominal strength is used to stabilize the pelvis and spine.

Shoulder Bridge 2 (BC7)

Use starting position guidelines as for Shoulder Bridge 1. This time place the Chi Ball between your knees. Ensure you make the same postural awareness adjustments as before. Breathe in, breathe out, flatten your navel to your spine and raise your pelvis off the floor, ensuring the body is elongated and the heels are pressing down into the floor.

Breathe in, breathe out in three short bursts as you squeeze the Chi Ball between your knees. Repeat twice more before lowering your spine, vertebra by vertebra, down to the floor. (Imagine your spine is a string of pearls.)

Benefits

Tones buttocks, back of legs, inner thighs, strengthens whole spinal column and postural support muscles. Abdominal strength is used to stabilize the pelvis and spine.

Half Roll Up with Spinal Extension (BC8)

Lie on your back with your knees bent. Place the Chi Ball between or just below your shoulder blades, which will lift the shoulders from the floor. Have a neutral pelvic position: pubic bone is level with your navel (avoid flattening the low back or dropping your waist), hips are even. Reach your hands to your knees to move the shoulder blades towards your hips, as if trying to connect them to your hips.

Clasp your hands behind your head. Breathe in, breathe out and draw your navel to your spine, then lift your upper body slightly off the Chi Ball. Breathe in to lift a little further, breathe out and lower your upper body and slightly arch your upper back over the Chi Ball. Make sure your lower back does not arch. Retain a neutral, flat pelvis. Only arch as far as your spinal flexibility and stability will allow.

Benefits

Strengthens the abdominals, promotes flexibility in the middle spine (thoracic spine), while also retaining stability in the lower back and pelvis.

Single Leg Stretch (BC9)

With knees bent, roll to one side and place the Chi Ball between your shoulder blades. Draw one knee at a time over the hips. Breathe in, breathe out and hollow the abdomen, raise your body weight slightly off the Chi Ball and rest your hands on your knees. Make sure the neck follows the line of the spine and the shoulders continue moving towards the hips throughout the exercise.

Breathe in, then breathe out to straighten your right leg, extending your hands to your left ankle, keeping your ankle in line with your knee. Breathe in, breathe out to change legs.

Repeat, alternating 8 to 10 times on each leg.

Benefits

Strengthens and tones abdominals, hips, stretches buttock and rear leg muscles. Disciplines and trains upper postural stabilizing muscles in the shoulder girdle.

Single Leg Circles (BC10)

Lie on your back and place the Chi Ball underneath your right ankle. Breathe in, breathe out and bend your left knee over the hip.

Press your right ankle firmly down into the Chi Ball without locking the knee joint. Ensure you have all other postural alignments checked: neutral pelvis, ribs down, shoulders sliding downwards, neck long. Breathe in again, breathe out and slowly circle your leg outwards without any of the following deviations in posture: waist twisting, hips rocking, ribs or shoulders lifting.

Execute 4 circles clockwise and 4 anticlockwise. Breathe in, breathe out and lower your leg. Repeat with the right leg circling.

Benefits

Strengthens and tones abdominal muscles, backs of the legs; mobilizes and strengthens muscles around the hip joint.

a
b

c
d

Side-Lying Leg Kick (BC11)

Lie on your right side, place the Chi Ball underneath your ankle and press it firmly into the floor with both legs.

Check that your knees, feet and hips are facing forward, and in a straight line; the navel is drawn into the spine; waist is up off the floor; draw your ribs down towards your navel, shoulder towards hip. Breathe in, breathe out and draw the navel to the spine as you raise the top leg with the foot pointed and knee facing forward.

Breathe in, breathe out to extend the leg behind.

Breathe in to flex the foot and swing the leg forward.

Repeat 10 times on each side.

Maintain a side-lying posture throughout. Watch for deviations from your straight line base position or tension: lower back arching, ribs opening forward, hips or shoulders rolling forward or back, neck or shoulder tension.

Benefits

Stretches and tones the whole legs, buttocks and hips. Trains postural stability in a side-lying position.

Side-Lying Leg Lifts 1 (BC12)

Lie on your right side, place the Chi Ball underneath your ribcage.

Check that your knees, feet and hips are parallel and in a straight line. Breathe in, breathe out and draw the navel to the spine. Breathe in as you raise your upper body away from the floor, pressing the ribcage into the Chi Ball; breathe out to release, allowing the body to relax and stretch over the Chi Ball.

Benefits

Helps stretch and release the ribcage, brings awareness of ribcage action when exercising in side-lying positions.

Side-Lying Leg Lifts 2 (BC13)

Lie on your right side, place the Chi Ball between your ankles.

Check that your knees, feet and hips are parallel and in a straight line and the waist is drawn up off the floor. Breathe in, breathe out and draw the navel to the spine as you raise both legs off the floor with the feet pointed and knees facing forward.

Concentrate on length, not height – it is far more beneficial to keep the legs quite low. Keep your left shoulder moving down towards your hip and all muscles engaged and in alignment. Breathe in to lower, breathe out to raise the legs.

Repeat 6 to 8 times on each side.

PROGRESSION

Raise both legs and torso off the floor, as below.

Benefits

All leg and postural muscles are engaged. Strengthens and tones inner leg, outer hips and waist.

a   b   c

Single Leg Lift (BC14)

Lie on your right side, place the Chi Ball underneath your ankle and press it firmly into the floor with both legs.

Check that your knees, feet and hips are facing forward and in a straight line; the navel is drawn into the spine; waist is up off the floor, your ribs drawn down towards your navel; shoulder towards hip. Breathe in, breathe out and draw the navel to the spine. Breathe in to raise the top leg with a foot flex, breathe out to point the foot and lower the leg.

Flex and point the leg 6 to 8 times.

Observe your posture throughout: keep the body long and stable.

Benefits

Stretches and tones the whole legs, buttocks and hips. Trains postural stability in a side-lying position.

Single Leg Kick (BC15)

Lying face down (prone), place the Chi Ball on the sternum bone. Place your elbows underneath your shoulders. Feel you are pushing the Chi Ball away from you with your chest. This elongates the spine and waist. Draw the shoulder blades down to your waist, roll the shoulders back and down. Extend your legs away, with feet pointed. Breathe in, breathe out, press your navel to your spine. Breathe in again and, as you breathe out in three short breaths, point your foot, flex it, then point it, gently bouncing your lower leg towards your buttock. Watch that the knee does not move from the centre line.

Benefits

Tones back of the legs, and buttocks. Teaches postural stability and discipline when executing movement in a prone position.

Swimming (BC16)

Lying face down (prone), place the Chi Ball on the sternum bone, then hug the Chi Ball with your body as you lower your head to the floor.

Breathe in, breathe out and draw the navel to the spine. Keep it firmly pressed there throughout. Breathe in again and lift the upper body. Feel that you are pushing the Chi Ball away from you with your chest. This elongates the spine and waist.

Draw the shoulder blades down to your waist, roll the shoulders back and down.

Breathe out as you turn your palm out and extend your right arm overhead.

Breathe in to stretch in this position, breathe out to bring the arm beside your body. Breathe in deeply, breathe out to lower and relax the body.

Repeat with the left arm.

Benefits

Strengthens the entire spinal muscles, shoulder girdle stabilizers for posture, shoulders and front of hips.

Half Plank (BC17)

Kneeling as shown, find neutral spine in cat position, with hands underneath the shoulders and knees immediately under the hips (see pages 48–49).

Breathe in, breathe out and press the navel to the spine without deviating from the neutral spinal position. Place the Chi Ball in the right hand, press down into the floor with the left hand, breathe out as you extend the right arm and left leg.

Breathe in, extending the body ball to toe, breathe out to raise the ball and foot off the floor.

Be aware of your posture. Have you sustained neutral spine and balance in the hips and shoulders? Take 3 to 5 full breaths in this position. Breathe in to stretch, breathe out to lower and change to the other side.

Benefits

Strengthens postural muscles. Teaches postural stability and spinal awareness.

145

The Lizard (BC18)

Put the Chi Ball between your feet, and lie face down with your knees bent and your elbows wide on the floor.

Driving your body and shoulders with your hands (just like a lizard!), breathe in and roll onto the left shoulder and allow the chest to lift while also lowering the Chi Ball to the floor on the left side of the body.

Breathe out and return to your start position and repeat to the right side.

Repeat, alternating right and left 8 to 10 times. Allow this exercise to be a relaxing, releasing one.

Benefits

Releases stiffness in the lower back area; mobilizes shoulder joints, ribcage, middle spine; stretches front of hips.

Torso Stretch (BC19)

Lie on your right side with your legs at a 90-degree angle to your body and your arms outstretched.

Take the Chi Ball in your left hand and draw a wide circle above your head. Allow the body to twist open.

Continue drawing 8 to 10 circles to release tension in the lower back, shoulders and neck.

Benefits

Good for relieving lower back pain and tension in shoulders and upper back.

Half Roll Down and Twist 1 (BC20)

Sit up straight with your knees bent and place the Chi Ball at the base of your spine; hold the side of your knees.

Breathe in, breathe out and press your navel to your spine and then release your body backwards, moving the lower back area first and squashing the Chi Ball behind you.

Breathe in to return to an upright posture with arms extended forward. Breathe out to bend your right elbow and twist the chest and waist to the right.

Keep the shoulders pressed down throughout; only twist as far as the sternum can.

Benefits

Strengthens and tones abdominal muscles. Promotes flexibility in lower and middle back; stimulates spinal nerves.

a   b   c

Half Roll Down and Twist 2 (BC21)

PROGRESSION

Prepare as for Half Roll Down and Twist 1. Execute with straight legs in either an upright position, with 'roll down', or with a 'twist'.

a   b

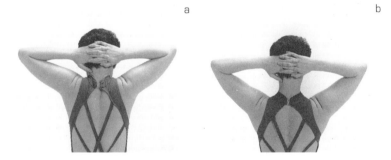

Scapular Elevation and Depression (BC22)

See page 49 for details of this movement.

Neutral Spine Position (BC23)

See pages 48–49 for details of this position.

Chi Ball Squeeze (BC24)

Lying face down, place the Chi Ball high up between your thighs. Rest your head on your hands and draw your shoulders down. Either keep your feet extended or flex them as shown. Breathe in; as you breathe out, press the navel to your spine and also squeeze the Chi Ball firmly between the thighs.

Try and use the base of the buttock muscles only, not the backs of your legs. As you squeeze, watch to see if you lose the navel-to-spine pressure.

Repeat 8 to 10 times.

Benefits

Teaches strength, stability and good postural alignment. Trains the abdominal muscles to support the spine; promotes correct abdominal action with breathing.

Chi Ball Method: Feldenkrais

In the energy cycle, Feldenkrais reflects Rising Yin and the Metal Element. After the heat-generating nature of Energize and Tone (Tai Chi/Chi Kung/Chi Ball Aerobic Dance) and the toning and muscle work during Yoga and Body Conditioning, the body is now warm, supple and ready to be stretched. We develop flexibility using Feldenkrais-based exercises in this section of Chi Ball, which relaxes and prepares the body for the final part of the class.

a

b

c

Side-Lying Shoulder Rock (F1)

Lie on your right side with your legs at a 90-degree angle to your body with your head resting on your folded arm.

With the Chi Ball in your left hand, keeping the arm absolutely straight push the Chi Ball away from your body, then pull it back towards you without bending your arm or breaking at the wrist.

Continue pushing the Chi Ball back and forth. Be aware of your shoulder and shoulder-blade movement.

Benefits

Relieves stiffness and tension in shoulder and neck. Re-awakens natural movement in upper back area.

Side-Lying Pelvic Rock (F2)

Position your body as for Side-Lying Shoulder Rock. This time place your Chi Ball between your knees. Try and push the Chi Ball away from the body with your hips.

Then draw your hip back, pulling the knee over the Chi Ball.

Keep the ankles and feet together and focus on the movement within the pelvis, lower back and waist. After several repetitions, notice if the upper body becomes integrated and active in the movement as well.

Benefits

Loosens sacrum, relieves tension and stiffness in middle and lower back muscles.

a   b

Butterfly Twists (F3)

Position your body as for the Side-Lying Shoulder and Pelvic Rocks. Place your Chi Ball between your knees. Clasp your hands behind your head.

Breathe in to open your left elbow to the side, breathe out to close.

Repeat this gentle twisting action 10 to 15 times. Make sure your knees are drawn right up in alignment with your abdomen. Avoid over-twisting, and each time use less and less effort to move. As you melt and relax, the body will soften and move easily and effortlessly.

Benefits

This gentle spinal twist rejuvenates and nourishes the spinal nerves.

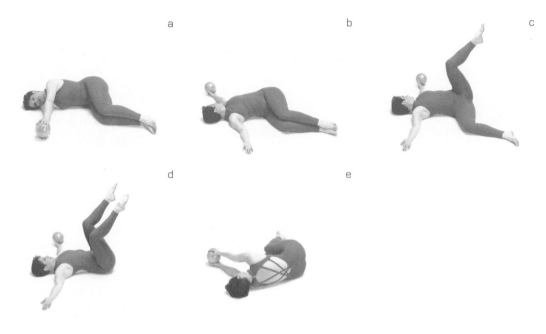

a   b   c

d   e

Space Roll (F4)

Position your body as for Side-Lying Shoulder and Pelvic Rocks (pages 151 and 152). Lie on your right side with your legs at a 90-degree angle to your body, with your head resting on the floor or on a pillow and both arms outstretched holding the Chi Ball.

Breathe in and take the Chi Ball across to the left side of the body.

Breathe out and chase the Chi Ball with your left, then your right leg, rolling your body on the floor until you are lying on your left side. Be relaxed and playful so that you melt and mould your body into the floor.

Benefits

Rolling on the floor massages and rejuvenates the whole body. It relieves mental and physical fatigue and promotes flexibility in the shoulders, chest, lower back and hips.

a   b   c

Pelvic Tilting (F5)

Lie on your back with your knees bent. Lift your pelvis off the floor and place the Chi Ball at the top of the pelvis just below the lower back area. Either raise your arms overhead or keep them beside your body.

Breathe in and allow the buttocks to fall over the Chi Ball so that the back arches.

Breathe out and use the feet to push the waist down towards the floor and feel the lower back flatten against the Chi Ball.

Avoid being overenthusiastic with this exercise. Be gentle and watchful throughout. Play with rhythm of quick and subtle to slow and more generous movements. Repeat 15 to 20 times.

Benefits

Releases stiffness and tension in the pelvis and lower spine.

Elevated Pelvic Tilting (F6)

Having first released the lower back and pelvis with the Pelvic Tilting exercise (page 155), raise your pelvis and hover just above the Chi Ball.

See if you can arch the back very slightly and round it, while staying slightly elevated.

Repeat 4 to 6 times before lowering your pelvis for 8 to 10 tilts on the Chi Ball. Repeat again with the pelvis elevated. When elevated, observe which areas of the body are also participating in this movement. As you become more relaxed, do you notice an increase of muscle participation?

Benefits

Will gradually release areas of the spine which have become immobile or stiff, improving fluidity in spinal movement.

a   b

Pelvic Circles (F7)

Version A – Mobilization: Lying supine with bent knees, position the Chi Ball at the base of the lumbar spine and at the top of the sacrum.

Begin circling your pelvis around the Chi Ball in a clockwise direction. Try keeping your knees stable and poised over the ankles throughout, so that the circles are driven by the pelvis rather than the legs. Avoid being too enthusiastic and overworking the muscles in the pelvis and lower back. Be gentle and watchful.

Repeat 15 to 20 times, then go anticlockwise. Notice any difference in the feeling of the movement. Rest for a minute or two before commencing the Elevated Pelvic Circles (see page 158).

Version B – Relaxation: Position your body and the Chi Ball as for Version A. Begin making quite large circles with your pelvis – about the size of a small dinner plate. After several repetitions, reduce the size of the circle to a small side plate, a drinks coaster, and then finally make the size of a large coin and have the navel area draw the circle. Try and feel this movement emanate right from the inner centre of your body.

After repeating each variation several times, return to the original largest circle. How does this circle feel now, compared to the first time you executed it? Notice any changes and then begin circling again, this time in an anticlockwise direction.

Elevated Pelvic Circles (F8)

Having first mobilized the pelvis on the Chi Ball, now press down into the feet and raise your pelvis and hover just above the Chi Ball.

Begin making tiny circles with your pelvis while hovering above the Chi Ball. Do 4 to 6 circles, then lower and make several relaxing circles on the Chi Ball.

Repeat this sequence 3 times before changing to an anticlockwise circle.

NOTE

If your feet are too far away from your hips you will feel excessive strain in the back of the legs. Make sure your feet are drawn in close to your buttocks.

Benefits

Gradually releases areas of the spine and spinal muscles which have become immobile or stiff, improving fluidity in spinal movement. Once full relaxation is achieved, the neck and shoulders are also massaged while elevated over the Chi Ball.

a   b

Pelvic Walking (F9)

Sit upright with the Chi Ball between your feet and hands beside your hips.

Try and make your right leg longer than your left by pushing your right foot forward.

Now make your left leg longer than your right. Practise slowly and smoothly and then gradually see if you can imitate a rhythmic walking action as effortlessly as you can.

Explore this movement for 3 to 5 minutes.

Benefits

Mobilizes the sacrum and releases tension in the lower back area. Good preparation for any forward bends or spinal twisting.

a   b   c

d   e   f

Lean and Look (F10)

Before you begin, see how easily or not you can stretch in this position by leaning forward. Execute each of the following exercise phases 10 to 12 times and bring yourself into an upright position after each variation.

Sit upright with the Chi Ball between your feet and hands beside your hips.

Begin by just lowering and lifting the head with natural ease.

Now lower the head and curve the upper spine as well.

Next lower the head, curve your whole spine and slide your hands along the floor towards your feet.

Next lower the head, curve your spine and look over your right shoulder.

Now lower the head, curve the spine, lean on your left hand and lift your elbow to look underneath your arm.

Finally, lower the head, curve the spine, lean on your left hand and extend your whole arm up and let your head follow your hand.

Lie down on your back to rest for 1 minute before repeating the whole sequence on the left side. When you lie down, notice if there is any change in the feeling in your back. When you have explored the left side as well, lean forward once again over your legs and observe any changes. Lie down again and see how your back feels.

Benefits

This sequence allows you to explore and improve your flexibility for the action of leaning forward without effort or strain. It encourages deviation from normal habit patterns that impede flexibility.

a   b

c   d

Side Lift and Look (F11)

First of all, lie down on your back and become aware of how you are breathing and how the body feels against the floor. Now roll onto your right side and place the Chi Ball between your knees.

With your left hand clasping your right ear, breathe in and lift your head off your arm without pulling or straining.

Breathe out and lie down again. Repeat 10 to 12 times. Lie on your back for 30 seconds before repeating on the other side.

Next place the Chi Ball underneath your ribcage.

Repeat lifting and lowering as before, 10 to 12 times each side.

Now lie down and observe your breathing. Has anything changed? Has the feeling in your back altered?

Benefits

Releases stiffness and tension in the ribcage, which impedes natural breathing. Promotes flexibility and mobility of the ribcage for sideways bending.

a

b

Neck Release (F12)

Place the Chi Ball at the base of the head.

Breathe in, breathe out and press your head down into the Chi Ball.

Breathe in to release, breathe out and again press down.

Repeat 6 to 8 times.

Benefits

Stimulates blood flow to the neck, shoulders and upper back muscles. Also stimulates the muscles along the spine. Stimulates acupressure points for relieving insomnia.

Neck Circles (F13)

Completely relax the head and neck and close your eyes.

Release the jaw, part the teeth and very slightly open your mouth. Begin making circles (about the size of an imaginary orange) clockwise with your chin. Next have your nose draw circles the size of a plum. Finally draw tiny circles the size of a cherry with the space between your eyebrows. Repeat each circle 8 to 10 times. Return to the largest circle and observe what you feel now, compared to the first time you executed this circle.

Repeat the whole routine anticlockwise. Observe: Are the circles perfectly round or is the movement chopping in certain places? Is the smallest circle you make shaking slightly (which is awareness of tension being held there) or is it smooth and relaxed? Breathe naturally throughout.

Benefits

Brings awareness of tension being carried in the neck muscles. A good exercise for slowing the mind down and releasing mental stress and tension.

a   b   c

d   e

Modified Fish (F14)

Place the Chi Ball in the middle of your back (thoracic spine), or just below the shoulder blades. If this feels too uncomfortable, air volume in the Chi Ball can be reduced to suit your spinal flexibility.

Have your legs outstretched into a wide 'V', then wrap your arms around your body and hug yourself tight. Begin rolling side to side on and off the Chi Ball. Allow the head to fall in the opposite direction to the elbows. Repeat several times, breathing in to raise the body onto the Chi Ball and breathing out to roll off to one side, as shown.

Next raise your arms above your body and extend the fingers to the ceiling. Breathe in as you raise both shoulders up; breathe out to drop both shoulders down towards the floor. Make sure this movement is smooth and not jerky.

As you breathe in, feel the body fill up and become active. When breathing out, feel the whole body sigh and release.

Next drop only one shoulder at a time, making sure the neck is completely relaxed, which will encourage more natural and intuitive movement of the upper body.

MODIFICATIONS

You can use a pillow or cushion to elevate your neck.

Benefits

Releases habitual stiffness and tension in the middle spine area (thoracic spine). Releasing this area of the spine also releases shoulder, neck and lower back muscle aches.

Breathing, Deep Relaxation and Meditation

Traditional Chinese Medicine and Yoga philosophies constantly affirm the advantages of conducting every activity of one's life (whether physical or mental) from a totally relaxed state. True strength, vitality and power are ours to enjoy when we think, move, feel and act from a completely relaxed state. This fifth and final part of a Chi Ball class represents the Water Element and is the period of Condensed Yin in the energy cycle, when we focus on relaxation, reflection and silence.

The other four phases are used to release as much tension from the body as possible so that stiffness, aches or pains will not interfere with the mind, allowing it to become an ocean of calm, stillness and peace. The Chi Ball Method uses three stages through which we practise achieving the ultimate goal of peace and happiness through relaxation: breathing exercises, Deep Relaxation techniques from Tai Chi, Chi Kung and Yoga, and Meditation based on the Zen style.

The journey to liberation from stress, tension and fatigue is approached through these three stages. By returning to a natural rhythm of breathing, the first band of tension is freed from the mind and body, making it easier for us to practise Deep Relaxation. Deep Relaxation provides the experience and practice we need to relax fully, in preparation for meditation. Meditation is the final stage for bringing balance and peace to the mind.

Breathing

Breathing exercises within the Chi Ball Method regulate our breathing pattern and rehabilitate diaphragmatic breathing – the first phase of relaxation. We cannot relax if our breathing pattern is tense and irregular, so we focus first on regulating and correcting it. For this we must learn full diaphragmatic breathing, which can be achieved by trying the following exercises.

Full Diaphragmatic Breathing

Either sit in a chair with the spine supported and absolutely straight, or lie down on your back.

a

b

Hara Breathing – Lying Down

Begin by placing one hand on the abdomen and one hand on the chest. Become aware of your breathing action. Try and keep the hand on the chest completely still, then focus on the abdominal hand and feel it move up as you inhale, and down as you exhale.

When you feel the chest is calm and still, place both hands just below the navel and breathe calmly and evenly, gradually lengthening the exhalation by counting 4 to inhale and 6 to 8 counts to exhale.

a

b

Hara Breathing – Seated

Stretching and Lengthening the Diaphragm

a   b

Has the Feeling in Your Back Changed?

Lying completely flat, feel the imprint of your back against the floor. Turn over and lie on your right side with the underarm stretched out above the head. Place the left hand on top of your head, lifting your head off your right arm.

Breathe in deeply and feel the underside of your ribcage push against the floor, and then against the Chi Ball.

Repeat 10 to 20 times.

Lie completely flat and see if there is any change in the feeling on that side of your back. Repeat on the left side.

Modified Head Balance

a   b   c

d   e   f

Has Your Breathing Rate Slowed?

Sit cross-legged on the floor and count the number of times you exhale in 1 minute. The purpose of this exercise is to reduce the number of exhalations per minute. As the number of breaths per minute is reduced (inhaling and then exhaling equals one breath), you may notice that your mind is more calm and relaxed.

Now turn over and kneel on your hands and knees (cat posture). Go down onto your elbows, which are shoulder-width apart and directly under your shoulders.

Clasp your hands together and then lower the crown of your head towards the floor, allowing the back of your hands to support the back of your head.

Breathe deeply for 10 to 20 breaths in this position. What parts of the back can you feel the breath is moving? Can you feel the undulation of the pelvis and lower back?

Now move your right knee towards your face – breathe 10 times.

Repeat with the left knee.

Breathe 5 times with both knees together.

Return to sitting cross-legged. Count again the number of exhalations per minute.

Straw Breathing

Has Your Mind Calmed Down?

The object of this exercise is to increase the length of the exhalation, which calms and relaxes the mind. Before commencing, count the number of exhalations per minute. Then, sitting comfortably on the floor or on a chair, pick up a long drinking straw and continue with the following exercise.

Inhale through the nose for 4 counts, exhale to a count of 8, through the straw. Repeat 4 to 6 times.

Inhale for 4 counts, hold for 2 counts, exhale for 8 counts, hold for 2 counts. Repeat 4 to 6 times.

Remove the straw and try to continue the slow, deep breathing.

Close your eyes and continue observing your breath. Every time your mind wanders, bring your concentration back to your breathing. Keep going for another 10 to 15 minutes, then open your eyes and be aware of the feeling you now have in your body and your mind. Try to keep that feeling with you as long as possible. Try and recall the memory of this feeling in times of stress and anxiety.

Deep Relaxation

Deep Relaxation is the second step towards peace and serenity. Relaxation where you slowly relax each and every part of the body makes you aware of final threads of tension which may be still lurking in the muscles, joints and nervous system.

Yoga Nidra

Yoga Nidra is about inducing relaxation by focusing on one body part at a time while relaxing in a chair or lying comfortably on the floor. If in a chair, the feet are flat on the floor (avoid crossing the ankles). Relax the hands in your lap, palms up, one on top of the other. If lying on the floor, in Corpse Pose (see page **128**) have the hands at an angle of about 30 degrees away from the body, palms up. Your legs should be straight along the floor (if the low back is 'pulling', place a pillow or blanket beneath your knees). Either record the following sequence onto a cassette tape or have a friend read it to you. Make sure while recording or reading it that your (or your friend's) voice is calm and soothing.

Simply call to mind each body part:

1   Right-hand thumb, first finger, second finger, third finger, fourth finger, palm of the hand, wrist, forearm, elbow, upper arm, shoulder, armpit, ribcage, waist, hip, thigh, knee, lower leg, ankle, sole of the foot, big toe, second toe, third toe, fourth toe, fifth toe. Now be aware of the whole of the right side of the body. Repeat same sequence on the left side.

2   Back of the body. Right leg, left leg, right buttock, left buttock, small of the back, right side of the back, left side of the back, whole spinal column, neck and the head – the whole head.

3   The forehead, right eyebrow, left eyebrow – eyebrow centre. Right temple, left temple – bridge of the nose. Right cheek, left cheek – tip of the nose. The jaw, the throat. Right side of the chest, left side of the chest – sternum. Upper part of the abdominals, lower part of the abdominals – navel. Right side of the hip, left side of the hip – pelvic centre.

4   Now feel the whole body against the floor. Whole of the right leg, whole of the left leg, whole of the right arm, whole of the left arm, the torso and the head – the whole head.

This sequence can be lengthened by allowing yourself to lie quietly for 5 to 10 minutes to fall deeper into the relaxation.

Using the Breath to Concentrate and Quieten the Mind

Lying comfortably on the floor in *Shavasana* (Corpse Pose; see page **128**).

1   First of all feel the air moving in and out of both nostrils as you breathe.

2   Slowly breathe in and feel cool air enter the left nostril and warm air leave the right nostril.

3   Now switch: slowly breathe in and feel cool air enter the right nostril and warm air leave the left nostril.

4   Now feel the air being drawn in through the left nostril once again, out through the right. Breathe in again through the right nostril and feel the breath leave the left nostril.

5   Now breathe again through both nostrils. Has the sensation within the nostrils changed or increased at all?

6   Is your breathing slower or deeper at all?

7   Do you feel more relaxed?

Remain in this relaxed state for a further 5 minutes to become fully aware of how you feel.

Returning from Deep Relaxation

1   Slowly increase the depth of your breathing.

2   Gradually draw your heels towards your buttocks.

3   Roll over onto your right side – away from the heart – and allow the forehead to fall forward onto the floor. Stay for 3 to 4 breaths.

4   Slowly sit up into a cross-legged position. Lift the arms above the head slowly 3 or 4 times to reawaken the body and the mind.

5   TAKE YOUR TIME STANDING UP AND RE-ENGAGING WITH YOUR DAY.

    To leap up straight after such deep relaxation virtually cancels out the experience. Dismantling stressful patterns will happen if you take the experience of the deeply relaxed state into your day and on into your life.

Meditation

Meditation can be the final and most profound step towards attaining balance, understanding, compassion and happiness, not just for ourselves but for those who share our lives – family, friends, acquaintances and working colleagues. When we feel more balanced and happy in ourselves, our lives will reflect the same back to us through the people we meet, experiences we have and opportunities which are presented to us.

Study each stage carefully to prepare yourself fully for practice. Make a commitment to meditate at least once a day. First thing in the morning is most beneficial, or immediately after your working day. Eventually twice a day for 20 minutes each time will consolidate and rebalance your chi. Take each day at a time. Keep a diary. This will help you become aware of insights and feelings about yourself which have been revealed to you by your mind during various meditations.

It is always extremely useful to seek professional guidance on how to meditate. Most cities or large towns have centres which run Yoga or Buddhist meditation sessions and/or weekend retreats.

Meditation is something you just have to try for yourself. Reams can – and have been – written about how to meditate and its many benefits. In the end you just have to sit and try it; nothing you read about it will really make sense until you do. What follows are three styles of meditation, from Tai Chi, Chi Kung and then Zen-style practice.

Tai Chi Standing Meditation

Standing meditation is an excellent discipline for relaxation and can be practised anywhere – when waiting for a bus or train, before an interview or presentation, first thing in the morning to prepare the mind for the day, and during the day to aid concentration and release stress.

1   Stand with your feet hip-width apart, soften the knees, straighten the spine and then sink the body weight into the heels.

2   (For women) Place your right hand just below the navel and the left hand on top; (for men) place your left hand just below the navel with your right hand over it.

3   Bring your attention to each of the following areas of the body, and relax them one by one:

neck

shoulders

arms

ribs

low back

buttocks

knees.

4   Now, half close your eyes and concentrate on your breath. With your hands still in place, feel them move outwards and away from your body as you inhale, and inwards as you exhale. Take at least 20 calm and relaxed breaths, extending this time to 10 or 20 minutes.

Chi Kung's Small Heavenly Circulation Meditation

This is a seated meditation that helps circulate the chi around the meridians of the Governing and Conception Vessels (see page **15**), balances yin and yang, and brings health and vitality to mind, body and spirit as all three become as one.

Using visualization, the chi is drawn from the perineum (a point between the anus and the external genitalia) up the spine to the crown of the head as you inhale, and down the front of the body as you exhale. To generate a continuous flow of chi, place your tongue on the roof of your mouth.

HOW TO PRACTISE SMALL HEAVENLY CIRCULATION MEDITATION

1   Sit comfortably in a chair with your feet flat on the ground, your spine straight and supported. Make sure your buttocks are pushed well back into the chair and your thighs are at a 90-degree angle.

2   Place the thumb of your right hand into the middle of the palm of your left hand, then softly clasp your hands together.

3   Close your eyes and gently place your tongue on the roof of your mouth (touching the ridge just behind the gums and top teeth).

4   Sit and breathe normally 5 or 6 times, feeling the abdomen move out as you inhale, and in as you exhale.

5   Inhale and visualize a line of energy being drawn from the perineum past the sacrum (back of the pelvis) and up the spine to the crown of the head. Hold the energy at the crown of the head for 2 counts, then slowly exhale and allow the line of energy to travel down the front of your body past the heart and navel and back to the perineum. Repeat this cycle 9 times, then relax and breathe normally,

keeping the tongue pressed to the roof of your mouth. Using visualization, continue imagining the circle of chi travelling up your spine to the crown and down the front of your body. Stay with this cycle for several minutes.

6   Now relax and just feel. What can you feel? Are you aware of any warmth or heat? Is one particular part of the body making its presence known? Observe the breath, remain relaxed and just feel.

7   Slowly open your eyes and, as you move gently away, take the feeling of the meditation with you.

WARNING

If you feel dizzy or uncomfortable during the breathing/visualization exercise, stop immediately, breathe normally and just relax. This can be due to your breathing still being a little tense and disorientated. Slow, regular and sympathetic practice will overcome initial difficulties. If not, please seek professional medical advice.

Chi Ball Zen-Style Meditation

Breathing is a means of awakening and maintaining full attention in order to look carefully, long and deep, see the nature of all things, and arrive at liberation.

Thich Nhat Hanh

If you have never meditated before, please reread the section entitled 'Meditation to Balance the Mind' (beginning on page **65**).

In this meditation practice we will continue to follow the principles of yin and yang by integrating sitting (yin) with movement (yang), adding a unique component not used in formal meditation practices.

The body is a storehouse of blocked memories and experiences. This style of meditation gives us the opportunity to release the thoughts and feelings that come to the surface of the mind, as well as releasing aches and pains.

The following instructions will prepare you for seated meditation:

POSTURE

Make sure you are really comfortable. Sit on the floor or, if this is uncomfortable, sit on a high cushion and support your knees, if necessary, with extra pillows. Place a soft towel under your ankles for extra comfort. Make sure the spine is straight.

Alternatively, sit in a chair with your feet apart, making sure your thighs are at a 90-degree angle to the floor. (Use a low stool or a couple of telephone books beneath your feet if necessary.) Make sure your spine is straight and supported.

BECOME AWARE OF YOUR BREATHING

Close your eyes and use the following breathing exercise to lengthen and become aware of your exhalations:

- Breathe in for 4 counts, breathe out for 4 counts.
- Breathe in for 4 counts, hold for 2 counts, breathe out for 4 counts, hold for 2 counts.

- ☯ Breathe in for 4 counts, hold for 2 counts, breathe out for 6 counts, hold for 2 counts.
- ☯ Breathe in for 4 counts, hold for 2 counts, breathe out for 8 counts, hold for 4 counts.
- ☯ Now breathe normally and relax the mind. If your attention wanders, bring it back to concentrate on your outgoing breath.

WATCH YOUR MIND

Allow thoughts that arise to float in and across the mind. As soon as you begin thinking about everyday chores, focus again and again on your outgoing breath.

LET GO

Do not focus on what you are feeling, just experience it. Dare to be vulnerable. Stay with the breath.

STAY WITH THE BREATH

Disturbing thoughts and feelings may come to the surface of the mind and affect the breathing. Be aware of losing track of your outgoing breath. Focus and almost sigh as you EXHALE, which is the natural way of responding to and releasing emotions which may overwhelm you.

HAVE NO EXPECTATIONS

The six emotional layers we discussed earlier (see pages **70–76**) may not be peeled back all at once. They are more likely to reveal themselves over a period of time, after we have been practising for some time. Sometimes you may feel calm, relaxed and very centred; at other times you may not. With each day we change physically, mentally and emotionally. Meditation teaches us to accept and deal with whatever is being presented to us on that particular day. Just observe and breathe.

LEAVING THE MEDITATION

At first you may want to set a clock for the amount of time you want to meditate. Eventually you will be able to sit for however long the meditation takes. When your timer beeps, switch it off and remain calm and still for a further 2 or 3 minutes. Slowly unfold your legs and wait. If you are sitting on the floor, move onto your hands and knees and slowly stand up and stretch. If you are in a chair, stand and raise your arms above your head and stretch the body.

The Practice

What follows are four levels or choices of Chi Ball Zen-style meditation, designed to bring balance to the mind and body. This unusual format of sitting (yin) combined with moving (yang) offers an opportunity for unification and integration of mind, body and spirit. Before commencing, be aware of the following:

- Become completely familiar with each suggested Chi Ball exercise prior to the meditation practice of your choice, and fully commit it to memory.
- Avoid any talking, continue the sitting discipline of following the outgoing breath, and try not to contribute to internal 'conversation'.
- Remain silent throughout. Be alert and attentive in both the meditative and movement sequences.
- Only music without vocals can be used for the movement practice.
- Prepare the body for seated meditation by gently stretching and releasing the body to release residual stiffness and tension with preparatory exercises such as Tai Chi moves The Butterfly, Circle-the-Sun and Circle-the-Moon (beginning on page **80**), Chi Kung's Press the Sky, Twist and Look and Heaven and Earth (beginning on page **89**), Yoga's Triangle Pose, Seated Forward Fold, Head to Knee, Cobra and Spinal Twist (beginning on page **107**), or Feldenkrais exercises Neck Release, Neck Circles and Modified Fish (beginning on page **151**).

CHOICES FOR DAILY PRACTICE

	Begin with	Followed by	Sequence repeated
1	A: Sit and observe the the breath for 5 minutes	B: Stand and practise Chi Ball Tai Chi moves (TC 1, 2, 3) to the left and right for 5 minutes	Practise A & B twice
2	A: Sit and observe the breath for 10 minutes	B: Stand and practise Chi Ball Tai Chi moves (TC 1, 6, 7) to the left and right for 10 minutes	Practise A & B twice

| 3 | A: Sit and observe the breath for 15 minutes | B: Stand and practise CK 1–4 OF Chi Ball Chi Kung Eight Brochades (page **37**) for 5 minutes | Practise A & B twice |
| 4 | A: Sit and observe the breath for 20 minutes | B: Stand and practise CK 1–8 of Chi Ball Chi Kung Eight Brochades for 10 minutes | Practise A & B twice |

CHOICES FOR EVENING OR WEEKEND PRACTICE

	Begin with	**Followed by**	**Sequence repeated**
1	A: Sit and observe the breath for 10 minutes	B: Stand and practise Chi Ball Tai Chi moves (TC 7, 5, 8) to the left and right for 10 minutes	Practise A & B three times
2	A: Sit and observe the breath for 15 minutes	B: Stand and practise CK 1–8 of Chi Ball Chi Kung Eight Brochades for 5 minutes	Practise A & B four times
3	A: Sit and observe the breath for 20 minutes	B: Stand and practise CK 1–8 of Chi Ball Chi Kung Eight Brochades for 10 minutes	Practise A & B three times
4	A: Sit and observe the breath for 30 minutes	B: Stand for 10 minutes of Chi Ball Tai Chi moves (TC 1, 8, 3, 4, 7) followed by a series of yoga postures to stretch and mobilize the body (Y 1, 3, 10, 4, 13, 14, 15, 16, 18) for 20 minutes	Practise A & B three times

HALF-DAY PRACTICE FOR EXPERIENCED MEDITATORS

	Begin with	Followed by	Sequence repeated
1	A: Sit and observe the breath for 20 minutes	B: Stand and practise CK 1–8 of Chi Ball Chi Kung Eight Brochades (page **37**) for 10 minutes	Repeat A & B four times
2	A: Sit and observe the breath for 30 minutes	B: Stand for Chi Ball Tai Chi moves (TC 1, 8, 6, 5) followed by 30 minutes of yoga standing (S) and seated (SD) postures: (S) Y 1, 2, 3, 4, 5, 6, 7, 9; (SD) 12, 13, 15, 14, 16, 18, 20	Practise A, B, C & D as a consecutive sequence
	C: Sit and observe the breath for 30 minutes	D: Practise 30 minutes of yoga standing (S) and seated (SD) postures: (S) Y 1, 2, 3, 4, 5, 6, 7, 9; (SD) 12, 13, 15, 14, 16, 18, 20, 21	

The Chi Ball Method uses the Five Elements theory to create a picture of balance throughout the year. Taking each element, the theory of creating and controlling cycles, and various exercise disciplines, we can build our own unique and individual platform for health. Working with the body will also contribute to balancing the mind and emotions.

What follows is an example, season by season, in approximately 10-week cycles, of how the Chi Ball Method uses the various energies of each of its exercise disciplines to express the Five Elements precept. This precept can of course also be applied to other exercise formats. Examples will be given for both Chi Ball and non-Chi Ball users.

First of all we have to divide the year up into its five seasons over 52 weeks of the calendar year. As the seasons move and change, so do we change the style and intensity of our exercise programmes.

Although the theme here is a seasonal one, whatever the time of year a practice will always encompass the yin/yang energy cycle. Each session will begin with a Rising Yang aspect, and finish with Condensed Yin – which ensures balance and rejuvenation.

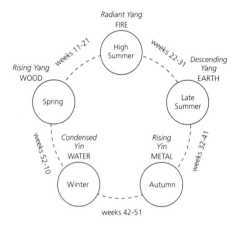

Creating Cycle of Energy from Season to Season, Element to Element: Northern Hemisphere

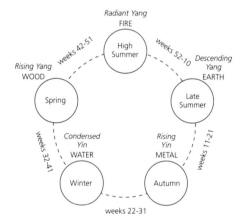

Creating Cycle of Energy from Season to Season, Element to Element: Southern Hemisphere

You will begin to see that at certain times of the year it is more appropriate to be more gentle with your exercise, while at other times vigorous physical exercise is encouraged.

In Spring, the main theme of a Chi Ball practice will be meridian-related and reflects the Wood Element. At this time of year the focus would be on all three aspects of Energize and Tone: Tai Chi, Chi Kung and gentle Chi Ball Aerobic Dance movements.

In Summer, more vigorous 'energize and tone' sequences plus Yoga exercises are done.

Late Summer concentrates on strength exercises in Yoga and Joseph Pilates' techniques.

Moves based on Feldenkrais predominate during the Autumn.

In Winter we use warming Yoga and Body Conditioning and Meditation to emulate the hibernation and stillness of Winter, which is aimed to conserve and rejuvenate our energies for the coming Spring.

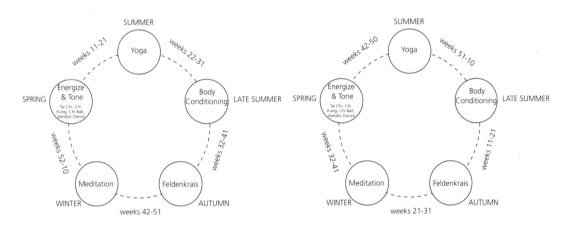

Creating Cycle of Energy from Season to Season, Element to Element: Northern Hemisphere

Creating Cycle of Energy from Season to Season, Element to Element: Southern Hemisphere

For those who prefer to work without a Chi Ball, I have offered alternatives which are aligned with the more classical forms of Tai Chi, Chi Kung, Yoga, Pilates® and modern exercise formats that encompass abdominal and back-strengthening exercises, stretching and relaxation. I have not described the aspects of each of these other disciplines for you, but I have supplied a recommended reading list so you can get more information on each of these topics (see page **206**).

Understanding more about any of them can be useful; I frequently use Chi Kung and basic Yoga exercises to relieve an aching back after long-distance travel, and find gentle Tai Chi and Yoga stretches help when recovering from a cold.

Please bear in mind that these are guidelines only. Always tune in to, and adhere to, your own energy levels before exercising. If you are tired or suffer severe ill-health, treat your body and energy with respect. Less really can be more and, in any case, 10 minutes a day for a year is 60 hours of exercise — a hugely positive contribution to your health. Be patient, as the best results are usually those accumulated over a long period of time.

Spring – The Wood Element

Element	Wood
Colour	Green
Season	Spring
Aspects of the creating cycle	Water, wood, fire
Aspects of the controlling cycle	Earth, metal
Chi Ball exercise elements	Standing meditation, Energize and Tone (Tai Chi, Chi Kung, Chi Ball Aerobic Dance), Yoga, Body Conditioning, Feldenkrais/Deep relaxation
Modern exercise elements	Breathing exercises, gentle to brisk walking, Yoga, resistance training, or Body Conditioning, stretching

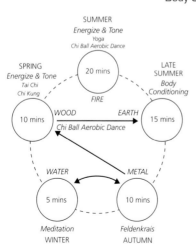

Seasonal Exercise Energy Cycle: Spring

As days lengthen and the temperature rises (Rising Yang) in Spring, aligning our exercise schedule with that of nature can be easy. Flowers budding and green leaves sprouting invariably motivate us to exercise, as does the prospect of revealing more bare skin during the Summer.

At this time of year a one-hour Chi Ball Method practice would begin with 10 minutes of gentle breathing or a standing Meditation followed with Energize and Tone sequences from Tai Chi- or Chi Kung-based movements and gentle Chi Ball Aerobic Dance sequences (Rising Yang). To follow we would spend 20 minutes doing standing Yoga postures to stimulate the chi and create warmth in the body (Radiant Yang). Fifteen minutes of Body Conditioning would then help to cool the body slowly and consolidate the chi (Descending Yang). Ten minutes of Feldenkrais-based exercises to release residual tension are combined with resting quietly for 5 or more minutes.

Alternative Exercise Format for Spring

Remember, it is not essential to have a Chi Ball to follow these exercise ideas. You can create a sequence that uses classical Tai Chi forms for 10 minutes, followed by a gentle walk outdoors (preferably in a park or along country footpaths). Use simple Yoga postures to promote strength and stability in the legs, followed by abdominal exercises to strengthen the back and front of the body. Complete your routine with gentle stretching and a 5-minute standing Meditation (see page **173**).

Summer – The Fire Element

Element	Fire
Colour	Red
Season	Summer
Aspects of the creating cycle	Wood, fire, earth
Aspects of the controlling cycle	Metal, water
Chi Ball exercise elements	Energize and Tone (Chi Kung, Chi Ball Aerobic Dance), Yoga or Body Conditioning, Feldenkrais, Deep Relaxation

Modern exercise elements   Chi Kung exercises, brisk walking or Yoga, abdominal exercises, or Body Conditioning, stretching, Deep Relaxation

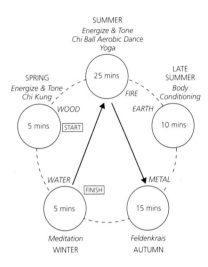

Seasonal Exercise Energy Cycle: Summer

Because this is the season of passion, abundance and high energies we should flourish physically, mentally and emotionally. A Chi Ball class would start with 5 minutes of sequences based on Chi Kung (Rising Yang) to stimulate the breathing and chi in preparation for the more physically demanding aerobic exercise to follow, which will challenge the cardio-respiratory system – the heart and lungs. We dance and move using Energize and Tone sequences for at least 25 minutes, creating immense heat as the blood is pushed through the muscles and chi is encouraged along the meridian system. Following this we spend 10 minutes on standing Yoga postures linked into a sequence to bring control to the breathing and maintain the heat (Radiant Yang).

Fifteen minutes of Yoga and Body Conditioning done on the floor now consolidate the rewards of the aerobic exercise – enhanced breathing and fewer pockets of tension (Descending Yang), and another 15 minutes of Feldenkrais-based moves then promote the flexibility that a warmer, more supple body will now allow (Rising Yin). We always finish with 5 to 10 minutes of Deep Relaxation/Meditation to cool the heat generated (Condensed Yin).

Alternative Exercise Format for Summer

Sequences without a Chi Ball would include the Chi Kung eight brochades (a sequence of eight movements that stretch and stimulate every meridian in the body – see page **89**), followed by Ashtanga-style Yoga abdominal strengthening exercises or Body Conditioning mat work exercises. Fifteen minutes of Feldenkrais exercises release the spine and hips, or you could try floor-based Yoga stretches to complement the metal aspect of this season, followed by 10 minutes of stillness and silence in the Yoga Corpse Pose.

Late Summer – The Earth Element

Element	Earth
Colour	Yellow
Season	Late Summer
Aspects of the creating cycle	Fire, earth, metal
Aspects of the controlling cycle	Wood, water
Chi Ball exercise elements	Energize and Tone (Chi Kung), Yoga, Body Conditioning, Feldenkrais, Deep Relaxation
Modern exercise elements	Chi Kung, Yoga or brisk walking, resistance training, or Body Conditioning, gentle stretching

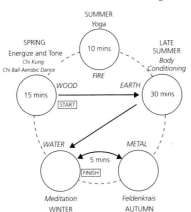

Seasonal Exercise Energy Cycle: Late Summer

In Late Summer we are starting to feel energetic, strong and confident because nature has plateaued, relaxed and surrendered to the Descending Yang energy. At this time of year we begin a Chi Ball class with 15 minutes of Chi Kung-based breathing exercises (Rising Yang) combined with a sequence of standing Yoga postures (Radiant Yang) to create heat and stimulate breathing. After this we spend 30 minutes doing floor-based Yoga sequences and Body Conditioning moves to strengthen the back and abdominals (Descending Yang). Feldenkrais exercises to release tension in the pelvis, spine and neck (Rising Yin), plus a short relaxation sequence (Condensed Yin), end the class.

Alternative Exercise Format for Late Summer

Chi Kung's eight precious exercises (see page **89**) and Yoga's Sun Salutation are ideal sequences to use in Late Summer. Body Conditioning mat work exercises perfectly balance the energetic sun salutation sequence and keep the breathing stimulated and engaged. Use gentle stretches, combined with breathing, for the neck, back, and hamstring and neck muscles as an alternative to Feldenkrais exercises. Make sure you release and relax the body entirely after asking it to work so energetically.

Autumn – The Metal Element

Element	Metal
Colour	Grey or metallic
Season	Autumn
Aspects of the creating cycle	Earth, metal, water
Aspects of the controlling cycle	Fire, wood
Chi Ball exercise elements	Energize and Tone (Tai Chi), Yoga, Body Conditioning/Feldenkrais, Deep Relaxation
Modern exercise elements	Tai Chi, Chi Kung or Yoga Sun Salutation, Body Conditioning/gentle stretching, or Deep Relaxation

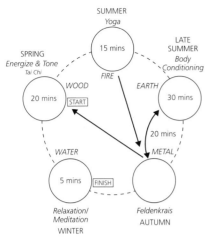

SUMMER
Yoga

(15 mins)

FIRE

LATE
SUMMER
*Body
Conditioning*

SPRING
Energize & Tone
Tai Chi

WOOD

(20 mins) [START]

EARTH

(30 mins)

20 mins

METAL

WATER

(5 mins) [FINISH]

*Relaxation/
Meditation*
WINTER

Feldenkrais
AUTUMN

Seasonal Exercise Energy Cycle: Autumn

As temperatures fall and the evenings draw in, our motivation to exercise is less apparent. We need to begin by warming the body, so we use Tai Chi to stimulate the circulation (Rising Yang). After 20 minutes we move onto gentle, fluid Yoga combined with Chi Ball Aerobic Dance sequences to generate warmth (Radiant Yang), during the 15 minutes of which muscles are stretched and joints mobilized. The focus of the class, with 20 minutes of Body Conditioning and Feldenkrais moves, then follows (Descending Yang and Rising Yin), before we end with a 5-minute relaxation. It should be noted that, in keeping with nature, the closer to Winter we come, the slower and more gentle the class becomes.

Alternative Exercise Format for Autumn

Although outdoor Tai Chi and Chi Kung are encouraged, advice from Tai Chi and Chi Kung masters is to avoid practice in adverse weather conditions. In Autumn, exposure to cold after the warmth of Summer will affect the lung energy and make us susceptible to colds and flu. Transferring your practice indoors would be preferable at this time of year. Begin with Tai Chi and follow it with Chi Kung's eight brochades (see pages **80** and **89**) or a short sequence of Yoga's Sun Salutation. Follow this with some abdominal or Body Conditioning exercises, combined with gentle stretching or floor-based Yoga work. Relax for 5 minutes or more.

Winter – The Water Element

Element	Water
Colour	Dark blue
Season	Winter
Aspects of the creating cycle	Metal, water, wood
Aspects of the controlling cycle	Fire, earth
Chi Ball exercise elements	Energize and Tone (Tai Chi, gentle Chi Ball Aerobic Dance), Yoga, Body Conditioning, Breathing exercises and Meditation
Modern exercise elements	Tai Chi, Chi Kung or Yoga standing postures, Yoga floor poses/Body Conditioning, Breathing exercises and Meditation

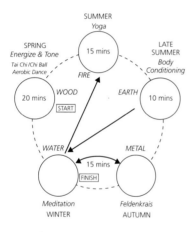

Seasonal Exercise Energy Cycle: Winter

Although a time of rest and rejuvenation, the body also needs warmth during Winter. Our Chi Ball session reflects this need. We spend the first 20 minutes in Tai Chi-based moves (Rising Yang) and in the 15 minutes that follow we do gentle, moving Yoga postures (Radiant Yang). Floor-based Yoga moves will also help to generate heat in the kidneys – one of most vulnerable organs at this time of year. Ten minutes of Body Conditioning back exercises (Descending Yang and Rising Yin) are added here; then, rather than lying down for relaxation, we introduce breathing exercises followed by seated and moving meditation. These two perfectly reflect the need for silence and stillness (Condensed Yin) in Winter.

Alternative Exercise Format for Winter

Begin with Tai Chi and follow with a sequence of four or five Yoga standing postures. Take to the floor and continue with some Yoga-based back bends (such as Bridge Pose or Cobra). Alternatively you can use Body Conditioning exercises that work specifically on the abdominals and back muscles – any of the exercises used in most modern exercise programmes for the back and abdominals will do. Follow this with the Straw Breathing exercise (see page **169**) and a seated meditation. Eat warming foods such as stews, soups and steamed vegetables at this time of year.

Seasonal Exercising – A Simple Approach

Should you prefer, practise just one of the five exercise disciplines for the corresponding time of year. For example, do Tai Chi or Chi Kung in Spring, Yoga in Summer, Body Conditioning in Late Summer, Feldenkrais in Autumn and Tai Chi and Meditation in Winter. Should you decide to exercise in this way, you might find it useful to learn more about each discipline by reading or attending an introductory course.

Seasonal Exercise Elements

Season	Nature's Response	In Energy Terms	Chi Ball/Exercise Elements
Spring	New growth	Rising energy	Chi Kung
Summer	Full bloom	High/Peak energy	Ashtanga or Iyengar Yoga
Late Summer	Harvesting time	Consolidating, compounding energy	Body Conditioning
Autumn	Reducing	Waning energy	Feldenkrais/Restorative Yoga
Winter	Hibernation	Slow, silent energy	Tai Chi/Meditation

Each discipline, as mentioned earlier, contains the yin/yang energy cycle, so Yoga postures, for example, are heating and energizing as well as cooling and restorative. This ensures balance, whichever exercise regime you choose to do.

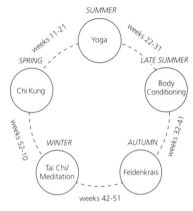

Seasonal Exercise Energy Cycle: Northern Hemisphere

chapter five

Mavis – Severe Neck and Shoulder Pain

Mavis was a nurse in her fifties who had suffered debilitating neck pain for more than 20 years. The pain was so great, she told me, that by the end of each day it had sapped all her energy and prevented her from getting anything approaching restful sleep during the night. I could see Mavis trying hard to look cheerful as she spoke, but her eyes and face told me that she was in a great deal of physical pain.

As we know, the first part of a Chi Ball class primarily involves moving the arms and upper body. The body warms up as the pace increases and we draw shapes in the air with the Chi Ball in our hands. Mavis said she did not think she was capable of doing these moves properly, but surprised herself by managing to do every one. As tension was released by moving her arms the moves got easier, and she was able to raise her arms higher and higher. After a while she began to smile and was obviously enjoying herself.

In the last stage of the class we used Feldenkrais-based exercises to mimic moves we did as children and to encourage playfulness. This releases stiffness and tension, particularly in the upper back, shoulders and neck. We began with shoulder rocking, pelvic rocking, butterfly twists and space rolls, finishing with the neck release and neck chi circles (see pages **151–65**) followed by 10 minutes of Deep Relaxation in the Corpse Pose (page **128**).

Six weeks later, having done two classes a week and practised at home, Mavis told me she had been able to sleep through the night without waking for the first time in 20 years. She astonished herself and her physiotherapist, who told her to carry on with whatever was giving her such profound relief.

The difference in Mavis's energy was obvious to anyone who knew her. She was transformed from a dull-eyed, drawn-faced and slumped-bodied woman into someone whose eyes shone as her shoulders relaxed, and she walked with her head carried high. Her whole personality had changed, and she exuded confidence.

Mavis eventually bought her own Chi Ball and continued to practise regularly at home and at work. She stands out as a perfect example of someone taking responsibility for their healing. Realizing we have the power to do this is the first step to accepting we in some way contribute to our own ill-health. All we have to do is reverse the choice from one of being sick and in pain to being healthy and well.

Suzanne – Weight Loss

Suzanne, a talented singer and musician, had suffered fluctuating weight problems since her teens and was in her early thirties by the time I met her. She had tried every diet plan, nutrition programme, exercise regime and therapy she'd come across, but her weight continued to fluctuate wildly up and down. Distraught and frustrated at continual failure, she believed she was 'way too fat' to be acceptable.

Weight problems are complex, and from my own experience I can see that the emotions play as large a part in our failure to be the weight we want as any type of dietary regime we follow. A saying which goes 'everything you focus your mind on expands' certainly seems to apply to our waistlines.

In the West we are completely obsessed by the size, shape and weight of our bodies. Around 30 years of the media-driven 'thin is best' message has done nothing to help the growing problem of obesity. By the time girls, and boys, are barely into their teens the message is engrained: unless you are pencil-thin you will not be accepted by society. The physical and mental consequences of this message are hard to undo.

I agreed to spend some time coaching Suzanne personally and we agreed to call the physical therapy sessions her 'feel-good' programme and forget any thoughts about how she might look afterwards. A positive internal change, such as concentrating on feeling good, tends naturally to reflect on our outside as well. We can look good, therefore, by default. How many times has an unexpected event, such as falling in love, getting a new job or being given a pay rise, resulted innocuously in weight loss? It happens, often because we feel better about ourselves – but also because our focus has been shifted from the shape of our body to how it *feels*.

Positive feelings lift and relax the spirit, which is then able to let go of whatever it clings to for survival – in Suzanne's case, extra fat. If we are continually and obsessively self-critical about our body, it automatically hangs on to what it has got, unsure of what sort of treatment to expect. Extra fat is stored, digestion is impaired, the functioning of our inner organs is hampered and our metabolism slows down. The circumstances are self-perpetuating.

Teaching Suzanne how to use exercise as a means of feeling good began gradually to dismantle the tension that was forcing her body to hold on to the excess weight. I also encouraged her to see a qualified Chinese herbalist and Food Energetics expert to assess and suggest changes to her diet.

All food, according to TCM practitioners, has its own type of energy which is described as being hot, cold, cool, warm or neutral. Mangoes, melons and tomatoes are examples of cold foods which should be eaten when the weather is warm, whereas in Winter we should eat warming foods such as leeks, onions, parsnips, blackberries and cherries.

Correct diagnosis of any inner imbalance and guidance on nutrition was another important part of bringing Suzanne's body back into balance. Food is the body's medicine, and each of us responds differently to certain diets. Health regimes such as vegetarianism, raw food diets or macrobiotic diets are not necessarily appropriate for everyone.

A depletion of energy in the spleen can be caused by what TCM refers to as a 'damp constitution' and is common in those who experience weight problems. A damp spleen, which ordinarily is a Fire organ helping to disperse moisture in the body, can be caused by overeating, too much fast food, drinking excessive quantities of cold liquid and eating too quickly, leading to water retention and feelings of slothfulness.

In this case, therefore, eating cold or raw foods and fruit could exacerbate the condition and slow the metabolism even further, so individual dietary assessment is important. I have found both TCM and Ayurvedic medicine (an Indian health practice whose principles serious Yoga students aspire to) effective in diagnosing and correcting serious and long-term health imbalances.

Initially Suzanne found it difficult trying to avoid feelings of frustration at not losing weight fast enough. Yes, we would all like to be a size 10 in three weeks! I banned her from weighing herself, and within six months her shape began to change. By the time she moved to Melbourne a year later, she had not only lost more than 14 kilos (30 lb) but the return of her vitality, energy and sheer enthusiasm for life meant she glowed with health.

She confessed in the end to disbelief that losing weight could be done in such a relaxed, natural and easy way. Like Suzanne, before the treatment most of us think we have to struggle and suffer to achieve anything, including the loss of a few extra pounds. Her example shows that we do not.

Leonie – Chronic Fatigue Syndrome

When 22-year-old Leonie started my classes in 1994 she had been suffering with Chronic Fatigue Syndrome for four years, which she believed was brought on by the stress of studying for her Master's degree. Within three months of doing the Chi Ball three times a week, Leonie had grasped the concept of the yin/yang energy cycle and how it related to her own condition, which followed a pattern of (rare) high-energy days and more frequent low-energy days.

As I have explained earlier in this book, CFS results when mentally, physically or emotionally we have overused or been too expressive with our yang energy – that is, worked too hard, thought and concentrated too intensively for too long, or exhausted our bodies through excessive physical activity. Although sufferers feel completely drained, the only recourse is the right sort of exercise therapy. Stagnant chi, which causes the feelings of exhaustion, needs to be stirred in order to take the individual from a state of sluggishness into one of deep relaxation.

Once her body became accustomed to the sensation of energy building up – which she would achieve during the three parts of a Chi Ball class (Energize and Tone: Tai Chi, Chi Kung and gentle Chi Ball Aerobic dance moves and Yoga postures) – followed by 20 minutes of Deep Relaxation to bring it back down, Leonie became much more sensitive to and aware of her energy threshold.

I suggested she scan her days, making a note of how much energy she had used and the number of hours she'd spent thinking, talking, eating, and generally being active. To counterbalance this I encouraged her to spend at least 20 minutes a day in Deep Relaxation. She eventually got into the habit of disciplining herself to relax whenever she felt fatigue setting in.

The first exercise involved lying on her back with her knees bent and rolling on the Chi Ball (which was under her neck) to release three key energy points along the spine: the sacrum (base of the spine), thoracic spine (just below the shoulder blades), and the cervical spine (top of the neck). This was followed by 5 to 10 minutes of lying completely flat on the floor, to allow the body to relax fully.

By removing the blockage of chi in the spine caused by stress, tension, poor postural habits and her emotions, Leonie was able to move more freely. Both exercises were completed with 10 to 20 breathing exercises and 5 minutes of lying completely still (Corpse Pose in Yoga).

I told Leonie that full recovery would take time. For every year during which we become ill we need a month of help or therapy to regain our health, say followers of TCM. Her mother contacted me 18 months after our sessions to say that Leonie was making steady progress, behaving with an awareness of how it might worsen her condition, and was in less of a hurry to meet her own get-well deadline.

Nursing Home Indigestion

A common problem among the elderly residents of a particular nursing home in Australia was indigestion and heartburn. After a number of chair-based Chi Ball classes, introduced into the home by one of the nurses, a resident said her indigestion appeared to be subsiding.

On hearing this the nurse gave each of those who attended the class a Chi Ball to place behind their backs as they ate and, before long, other residents were reporting less heartburn. Elevating the ribcage by placing a Chi Ball in the middle of the back (thoracic spine) took pressure off the diaphragm, allowing the residents to breathe properly as they ate and so helping their digestion.

Anne Marrie– Back Pain

The best way of illustrating registered nurse Anne Marrie's story is to reprint, with her permission, an edited version of the letter she sent me from Victoria, Australia on 8 October 1999. She had been advised, after years of lifting patients and subsequent chronic back pain, to have the discs in her spine removed. Despite surgical intervention, she continued to suffer immense physical, mental and emotional pain.

Dear Monica,

This is to compliment you on developing a most beneficial form of exercising, which is pleasant and fun. I am a registered nurse with many years' experience in acute medicine, which involves a lot of physical labour. I am now missing four discs in my back following two lots of surgery. I have tried to overcome my debilitation with exercise, such as swimming and water running.

I recently began going to some exercise classes where the teacher introduced us to Chi Ball. I found it very helpful and my spine began to improve. I decided to buy some balls of my own so I could practise at home, and then discovered your videos. I now use them every day – I particularly enjoy Chi Yoga, which I do just before bed or first thing in the morning. Your programme has improved by spine so much that I have recovered wonderful flexibility, and by the end of the exercise have lost much of the pain I suffer.

There are other benefits too that are slowly becoming obvious. I have lost my clinical depression, my confidence is returning, and I find everyday movement so much easier. My whole well-being is improving. I am so taken with what you have done that I recommend Chi Ball to many others, and three more of my friends are now proud owners of Chi Balls.

For my part, you have liberated my life. I mean that as strongly as I have stated. Please know that there must be many more of us out there you are helping. Warmest regards.

Anne Marrie

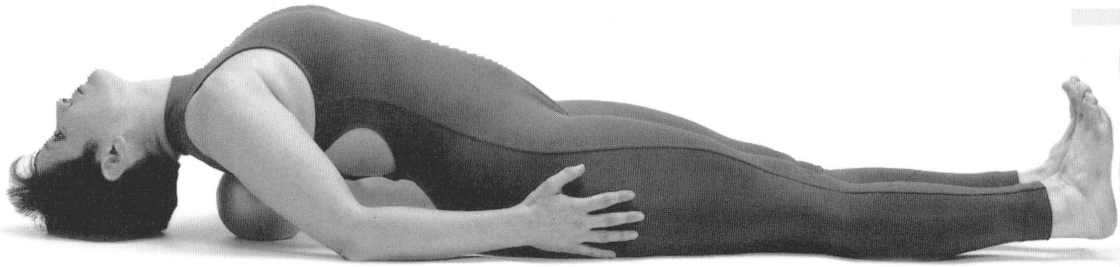

chapter six

living, listening and longevity

How and Why We Participate in Our Health

Most of us take our health for granted until something goes wrong. Only then do we start to question whether some aspect of our life or behaviour has contributed to our ill-health. The degree to which we investigate this matter and make any changes to the way we live depends on how sick we become. More often than not we go to the doctor, take some form of medication and, as soon as the problem has disappeared, revert to our normal habits.

Cultivating Awareness

Someone once told me in passing that having and not having awareness is the difference between drinking three bottles of red wine on a Friday night, knowing you will feel like hell the next day, and drinking three bottles of red wine while having no idea you'll feel like hell the next day. Without an awareness of the effects of our behaviour on our health, we can never achieve complete good health.

East vs West

Tai Chi, Chi Kung, Yoga and meditation are increasingly popular in the West, which is, I believe, because we are instinctively searching for more balance and better health. In those who try to integrate into their lives the philosophy behind these types of exercise, real improvements in the health of their mind, spirit and body begin to appear. These improvements, for most, have not been achieved by anything the West has to offer.

The main difference between Eastern and Western exercise formats is the *focus*. In the West we concentrate on the medical and scientific reasons for exercise and on how regular workouts make us look. We stretch at the beginning and end of a session to avoid injury, not because it happens also to be of huge benefit to our organs, brain, lymphatic system and in calming and quietening the whole body.

Like modern medicine, modern fitness compartmentalizes the body, breaking it up and exercising one part at a time. We are rarely asked to think about or use our bodies in the way they are made: as a whole. Once we do, the way we see ourselves, and the results that exercise starts to achieve, are profound.

The Importance of Listening to Our Bodies

According to practitioners of Traditional Chinese Medicine, we often receive warnings of impending sickness or injury six to nine months prior to when the injury or illness makes itself known. We ignore those irritating niggles, which are quite often the early signs of serious medical problems. There are countless stories of people who have ignored lumps, chest pains or severe abdominal cramps and ended up in hospital, or even dead.

Even catching a cold gives us the chance to think about our more general state of health. How has our immune system become weak enough to allow our bodies to become vulnerable to a cold or flu virus? The body's effectiveness can be worn down by overwork, eating too much processed food, breathing polluted air, excessive quantities of alcohol and lack of rest and sleep. Researchers in Sydney, Australia, recently discovered that adults and many children now suffer sleep deprivation, which the researcher linked to stress, depression and poor health. Within four to five days of catching up on their sleep, the subjects of this study had more energy, improved concentration and were less irritable.

But still the connection between the health of the body and that of the mind is largely ignored by medical professionals. They treat patients often as a collection of many distinct parts instead of connecting the many parts and treating the person as a whole. There are signs in certain areas that this attitude is starting to change, with some health-care workers seeing that Eastern and Western medicine can be complementary. I believe the same applies to exercise.

Western exercise can become Eastern in experience simply by shifting the focus from how we look to how we *feel*. We could start, in many gyms and fitness classes, by removing the mirrors. Watching ourselves and comparing the way we move with others in the class feeds our obsession with the body, externalizing the focus of a practice that should be concentrated and guided by the way we feel. Adding breathing, placing a greater emphasis on stretching, using exercises adapted from Yoga and having a larger part of the class be slower in pace, would all offer benefits to the modern aerobics class similar to those we derive from Eastern equivalents.

To create your own weekly East/West mind/body fitness regime, use the following as a guide:

Monday	Low-impact aerobics
Tuesday and Wednesday	Resistance training
Thursday	Power Yoga class
Friday	Body conditioning
Saturday	Stretch and relaxation
Sunday	Rest

How to Respond to Health Warning Signals

The world today seems to demand that we live at an ever-increasing pace. Somehow we manage to keep up, but for many the health costs can be great. If we are to enjoy greater health and control over our lives we must become more sensitive and obedient to our individual needs. This means resting when we are tired, indulging ourselves occasionally with treats, and setting even a small amount of time aside for a little fun.

To be able to do all this for maximum effect we must learn how to respond to our body's demands. Colds and flu, for example, are often preceded by several days of worry or stress. Instead of pressing on we should have a long soak in the bath, book an aromatherapy massage or practise some Deep Relaxation and Meditation.

Muscular tension in the shoulders and neck, emotional and mental pressures, or a malfunction of the liver and large intestine, can all be the cause of a headache. Yoga postures plus some relaxation can help to cleanse the organs and release tension in certain muscles.

Probably the most useful warning signs to heed are those associated with fatigue. These include an inability to concentrate, frequent emotional outbursts, insomnia, loss of appetite, poor post-exercise recovery and generally sluggish energy. Every other problem we might have seems worse when we are tired, just because we have neither the mental nor physical energy to deal with them.

Building regular periods of rest and relaxation into your daily life will help you to avoid ever becoming overtired, and allow every other part of your body and mind a better chance to stay healthy. Would you starve, neglect or overwork your best friend? Then why do it to yourself?

Our Natural State – Detachment

It can sometimes take years of disciplined practice before we see the impact regular meditation has on our lives. But, with time, it should teach all of us to return to our natural mental and emotional states of detachment.

This means not allowing ourselves to be emotionally dragged into the challenges life lays down, but rather to stand back and look at problems or difficulties from all angles before we respond. Having contemplated how we wish to respond, the problem itself, and our view of it, will often change dramatically. How different is our response, then, compared with the way we might have automatically reacted hours or days earlier?

We all tend to overlook the simple pleasures of life. Taking in and appreciating every single moment prepares us to fully embrace and cherish the smallest surprises. Miracles enter our lives when we have the peace of mind to be content and happy with everything just as it is.

Oriental Medicine

The Yellow Emperor's Classic of Internal Medicine Ilza Veith (ed.), University of California Press

The Yellow Emperor's Classic of Medicine Maoshing Ni, Ph.D., Shambhala

The Web That Has No Weaver Ted Kaptchuk, Congdon & Weed

Between Heaven and Earth – A Guide to Chinese medicine Harriet Beinfield, L.Ac., and Efrem Korngold, L.Ac., O.M.D., Ballantyne Publishing

Yin & Yang – Understanding the Chinese philosophy of opposites and how to apply it to your everyday life Martin Palmer, Piatkus

The Oriental Way To Health – A Self-help Guide to Traditional Chinese Medicine Dr Stephen Gascoigne, Simon & Schuster

9 Ways to Body Wisdom Jennifer Harper, Thorsons

Shiatsu-Du Ray Radolfi, British School of Shiatsu

How to See Your Health: Book of Oriental Diagnosis Michio Kushi, Japan Publications Inc.

The Ohashi Bodywork Book Watani Ohashi, Kodansha

Meridian Exercises – The oriental way to health and vitality Shizuto Masunaga, translated by Stephen Brown, Japan Publications Inc.

The Joy of Feeling Iona Marsaa Teeguarden, Japan Publications Inc.

Acupressure: How to Cure Common Ailments the Natural Way Michael Reed Gach, Piatkus

Healing with Foods: Oriental Traditions and Modern Nutrition Paul Pitchford, North Atlantic Books

Helping Ourselves: A Guide to Traditional Chinese Food Energetics Daverick Leggett, Meridian Press

Tai Chi

The Inner Structure of Tai Chi Mantak Chia and Juan Li, Tuttle Publishing

Principles of Tai Chi Paul Brecher, Thorsons

Chi Kung

Mastering Miracles Dr Hong Liu, Warner Books

The Art of Chi Kung Wong Kiew Kit, Element Books

The Way of Chi Kung Kenneth S. Cohen, Bantam Books

Chi Kung – Harnessing the power of the universe Daniel Reid, Simon & Schuster

Eastern Philosophy

Lao Tsu's Tao Te Ching Timothy Freke (ed.), Piatkus

Lao Tsu's Tao Te Ching Translated by John C. H. Wu, Shambhala

Yoga

Yoga for Stress Relief Swami Shivapremananda, Gaia Books

Yoga the Iyengar Way Silva, Mira and Shyam Mehta, Dorling Kindersley

Yoga Over 50 Mary Stewart, Little, Brown & Co.

Body, Mind and Sport John Douillard, Bantam

The Spirit and Practice of Moving into Stillness Eric Schiffmann, Pocket Books

Yoga Journal's Yoga Basics Mara Carrico, Owl Books

Dynamic Yoga Godfrey Devereux, Thorsons

Video tapes, courses and retreats

The Life Centre
15 Edge Street
London
W8 7PN
Tel: 020 7221 4602
Fax: 020 7221 4603

Ashtanga Vinyasa Yoga
The Practice Place
177 Ditchling Road
Brighton
BN1 6JB
Tel/Fax: 01273 276175

Iyengar Yoga Institute
223a Randolph Avenue
London
W9 1NL
Tel: 020 7624 3080

The Yoga Centre
16 Canning Street
Edinburgh
EH3 8EG
Tel/Fax: 0131 221 9697

The Kevala Centre (International Yoga School)
Tel/Fax: 01803 215678
Offers a Diploma course in Yoga by
correspondence.

Pilates®

'Spinal Stabilisation', Christopher M. Norris, *Physiotherapy: The Journal of the Chartered Society of Physiotherapy*

Feb/March 1995

Body Control The Pilates Way Lynne Robinson and Gordon Thompson, Box Tree

The Mind/Body Workout with Pilates and Alexander Technique Lynne Robinson and Helge Fisher, Pan Books

The Complete Guide to the Pilates Method Allan Menezes, Ahead in Marketing

Pilates' Return to Life Through Contrology Joseph H. Pilates and William John Miller, Presentation Dynamics Inc.

Stott Pilates – Canada

Moira Stott, www.stottconditioning.com

Feldenkrais

Awareness Through Movement Moshe Feldenkrais, Arkana

The Master Moves Moshe Feldenkrais, Meta Publishers

The Potent Self – A Guide to Spontaneity Moshe Feldenkrais, Meta Publishers

Mindful Spontaneity Ruthy Alon, North Atlantic Books

Practical Feldenkrais for Dynamic Health Steven Shafarman, Thorsons

Emotional Anatomy Stanley Keleman, Center Press, Berkeley

Discovering the Body's Wisdom Mirka Knaster, Bantam

Breathing, Deep Relaxation and Meditation

Breathe! You Are Alive Thich Nhat Hanh, Rider Publishing

The Breathing Book Donna Farhi, Owl Books

The Healing Power of the Mind Tulku Thondup, Arkana

Everyday Zen Charlotte Beck, Thorsons

Taoist Ways to Transform Stress into Vitality Mantak Chia, Healing Tao Center

The Miracle of Mindfulness Thich Nhat Hanh, Rider Publishing

Absolute Happiness – The Way to a Life of Complete Fulfilment Michael Domeyko-Rowland, Hay House

awaken your body

balance your mind

Monica Linford's Chi Balls can be ordered from:

International Fitness Promotions
PO Box 1592
Ascot
Berkshire SL5 OXD
UK

or

PO Box 542
Mitcham
South Australia 5062
Australia

or from www.chiball.com

index

awaken your body

balance your mind

nine ways to body wisdom

blending natural therapies to nourish body, emotions and soul

Jennifer Harper

Nine Ways to Body Wisdom skilfully blends the best of traditional eastern medicine and western natural therapies to create a powerful new way of working with your body.

The Nine Ways:

- nutrition
- herbs and spices
- exercise
- reflexology
- acupressure
- aromatherapy
- flower remedies
- affirmations, and
- meditations

combine to form the perfect self-treatment system.

Jennifer Harper N.D., Ph.D. is a qualified naturopathic doctor and herbalist who runs a successful clinical practice. She is also a popular broadcaster and media columnist.

Develop your own personal health plan you can follow throughout the year!

the big book of ch'i

an exploration of energy, form and spirit

Paul Wildish

This beautifully illustrated book takes a fascinating look at the origins of 'ch'i' – our 'living essence' and the vital energy behind healing practices like reiki, chi kung, acupuncture and shiatsu. When this vital force is sluggish or becomes blocked, our health suffers; these ancient Eastern healing practices were developed to clear such energy blocks and to restore harmony within the body. Martial arts, like tai chi and aikido, use this same vital energy for self-protection and health promotion through exercise.

Paul Wildish, a martial arts expert and a senior instructor for the British Aikido Association, has studied aikido, shiatsu and reiki. In *The Big Book of Ch'i* he introduces these traditional ways to awaken this energy force and fulfil our true potential.

dynamic yoga

the ultimate workout that chills your mind as it charges your body

Godfrey Devereux

Dynamic Yoga is an unbeatable form of exercise. Its dynamic workout combines fitness training with stress release in a scientifically devised sequence of flowing postures. This sequence of postures enable you to build up strength, flexibility, stamina, concentration and alertness.

Dynamic Yoga is an effective, simplified way to gain the far-reaching benefits of classical Ashtanga Vinyasa Yoga not available in many contemporary yoga styles. Every workout is fully illustrated with step-by-step instructions on how to move in and out of each posture safely and effectively.

Godfrey Devereux is the author of *15-Minute Yoga* and *Hatha Yoga*. He was the Yoga Director of the Life Centre in Kensington, London for three years, and now runs a Yoga Training Centre on the island of Ibiza.